STANDTALL

HOW TO LEAD FROM WITHIN AND CREATE HIGH PERFORMANCE TEAMS

JERON MASTRUD

Paperback ISBN - 9780999194911
Library of Congress Control Number – 2017959277
Published by eFluential Publishing, Roswell Georgia
info@efluentialpublishing.com
First Edition: October 2017
Printed in the United States of American

PRAISE FOR STAND TALL

"Stand Tall is a thoughtful & revealing look into the achievement oriented mind of Jeron Mastrud. On a team of 125 players & with dozens of professional staff in the Kansas State University football program, Jeron stood tall with his preparation & selflessness. This has continued in each chapter of his life. He is smart, tough, kind & focused. A winner.

"The Mastrud family has a culture of respect & hard work. Many families & business do. The thing that separates the Mastrud family is the service to others & attention to detail that they live by. Each member of our teams knew that Jeron Mastrud would prepare to do his job and he had their back with support & respect. People like Jeron make teams/organizations feel like family.

"Stand Tall is not only the story of a successful young man's journey but also, of the success process that the Mastrud family itself is renowned for. Any individual or group would benefit from the principles shared in this book. Jeron doesn't just believe in them, he lives by them."

Ron Prince, Offensive Line and Assistant Head Coach Detroit Lions

"I have enjoyed watching Jeron's natural leadership ability in high school, at Kansas State, in the NFL and now in his professional life. He embodies the type of person we look for in our student-athletes today by demonstrating consistency, determination and an ability to learn quickly. Jeron's positive attitude, great work ethic and willingness to sacrifice developed him into the fearless leader he is today. I have so much love and respect for the man he has become!"

James Franklin, Head Coach Penn State Football

"Jeron epitomizes the intrinsic core value system he has written about in this book. As a caring, genuine and sincere person he demonstrated quality, dynamic and demanding leadership with his teammates. Jeron is a committed young man: unselfish, self-disciplined, consistent, responsible, mentally strong and enthusiastic. He pursued daily self-improvement through great effort and persistence without placing any limitations on his ability to achieve success."

Bill Snyder, College Football Hall of Fame and Head Coach Kansas State Football

DEDICATION

This book, albeit my first, has taken far too long! There are a few people I would like to thank for pushing me to start, guide me through, and complete the project I'm proud to finally release.

Thank you, Annica Torneryd for giving me the "kick" to put this book out there to the world. Hearing all your experiences from being a single mother, to world kickboxing champion, to bestselling author made me realize that I have what it takes!

Thank you Cliff Pelloni for helping me get this from just an idea in my head to a finished book I can hold in my hand! It was hard for me to visualize something I've never done before and but you made it VERY simple! You kept me moving forward when I needed a push. This book would have never happened without your knowledge and expertise.

Thank you Kelly Fidel for the clarity and guidance throughout this project. You've help me always see the bigger picture and pushed me to achieve heights I may not have reached for on my own. Thank you for being my light on what sometimes seems like a dark, ominous path.

I would like to give a special thank you to my AMAZING parents, Brad and Dede. Almost every topic I touch on throughout the book stems from how you raised me. Mom, you taught me patience while Dad taught me perseverance. Dad you taught me toughness while Mom taught me kindness (still working on that!). Together you exemplify teamwork, leadership and fearlessness that I've admired every day from Roseburg to Beaverton and on to wherever else my life has taken me. I love you so much and had you in mind all throughout this book. I hope you like it!

CONTENTS

INTRODUCTION

"Do it with passion or not at all."

When I first sat down to write this book, I realized I jumped pretty quickly into some concepts and stories without giving much preface or background. My dad made me realize that not everyone has the same experiences I've gone through and that starting with a foundation would be more helpful and make things easier to understand. I sat on that comment for a couple months thinking about the fundamental reasons the fire inside me burns on its own, what drives my leadership of myself and of others, and where that even starts.

The following are three Ps: Passion, a Plan, and Perseverance. Without having an understanding of these three things, the rest of the book wouldn''t make as much sense. A burning passion, a detailed plan, and relentless perseverance have always been the cornerstones to my leadership and my desire to be great.

PASSION

A high level of success at something all starts with a passion for something. Not something you simply like to do or that pays the bills, but something that you're genuinely passionate about. Something that awakens you deep down and excites you at the very core. Something that almost feels a part of you. A passion doesn't necessarily define you, but when you find something you're deeply passionate about, it can almost feel that way.

I felt that passion for the game of football at the beginning of my sophomore year at my first varsity start. This was the first time I got to experience what it was like to play under the Friday night lights. My dad was a high school football coach. All my life I grew up going to his games every single Friday night. I'd witnessed multiple division one athletes, future NFL players, down-to-the-wire games, sold-out crowds and championship seasons. I'd even witnessed back-to-back undefeated championship seasons defined by pure dominance and excellence. Yet none of that sparked my inner passion for the game. It may have laid a solid foundation, but as soon as I took that field for my first varsity game (also with my dad as the head coach), I felt it. The first snap I had, I instantly wanted more. With each play, came more and more excitement and exposure to the highest level of football I'd experienced. I couldn't get enough. It was during my varsity season I realized this might be something I could be good at. Most importantly, it was when I realized a genuine passion for the game and sport of football.

Without that passion, the early morning workouts would've become a drag, the two-a-day summer practices would've been unbearable, and the constant physical strain would've made me want to quit. This happened for baseball. When the going got tough and the competition heated up, I realized I truly didn't want to proceed. But with football, that only compelled me more. The fire inside burned brighter and hotter. I welcomed any and all competition. I sought out extra workouts to refine techniques and enhance weaknesses. My whole life, football was the fuel to my flame inside. Then it ended. I was no longer playing, and my dad was no longer coaching. Something that had seemed to define my existence was abruptly gone without warning. But I've quickly realized, football didn't and doesn't define me. It was and still is a passion. I give back to my community now by coaching high school athletes. That still helps channel my passion for the sport. More importantly, I realized I'm just as passionate, if not more, about other aspects of my life.

Passion is something that, without a risk or new challenge, may seem impossible. Without passion, fear can succeed and keep you from reaching the goals you set out to accomplish. When passion is channeled correctly, and you're in a place and doing something you're genuinely passionate about, the success will follow. I've taken the time to reflect and find what makes that flame inside me burn on its own without the forced motivation from someone else or something else—including fear. And I found a variety of things...

I learned to ski at the age of three. I skied at least two weeks of every year until I turned eleven. Just as I was able to rip a black diamond run, I decided to join the then-new trend of snowboarding. I've looked forward to time on the mountain every winter. The first chairlift up the mountain for my first run of the season comes a feeling eerily similar to that of the first snap of a football game. When I took the time after my football career ended, and realized how fulfilled I felt when hitting the slopes, it made me understand more that I have found another passion equal to football in the sport of snowboarding.

I know—that doesn't count in your book because that's just another sport for an adrenaline junkie finding a new outlet. Maybe.

But then I was approached for the first time by someone in desperate need of a solution for chronic pain. This person's quality of life was severely diminished, and it impacted their ability to spend time with their loved ones, let alone enjoy an active lifestyle.

After only thirty minutes together, this person went from being unable to stand without a level 10 of 10 pain to walking around freely with no pain. It was remarkable. No pills. No injections. And no, it wasn't some voodoo magic. But the relief they felt wasn't anywhere close to the flame that was reignited inside me that made me realize I have a genuine passion in helping people and seeing them feel better. This brings me equal enjoyment to the opening game of a season (including on the road at Auburn or Sunday Night Football versus a division rival) or ripping a run on a bluebird, powder day on the mountain. And so it began, my passion to help others be able to enjoy the active lifestyle that I had for so long.

> *" People with great passion make the impossible happen."*

A PLAN

Many people think that football players work out a little bit, practice a little bit, and then just show up and play in front of a ton of people and are overpaid and over glorified. Man, that statement couldn't be more false. The intricacies and details behind every month, week, day...shoot, down to the minute,

9

are heavily accounted for. The critics may have one part right in stating that life is easy for a football player in the sense that your schedule is very well laid out for you and gives you little time on your own. The time on your own should be best spent to prepare, physically and mentally, for the agenda ahead.

There is a detailed plan laid out far in advance to lead a team to a Super Bowl. That may sound funny to the average person, but the only reason anyone is there is to win the Super Bowl and nothing else. If that doesn"t happen, then you'll be looking for a new job!

The importance of having a plan, and a detailed one, became even more important once my time in the NFL concluded. I was suddenly handed an abundance of time that I wasn't sure what to do with or how to best organize it to be successful in my next endeavor. I knew having a healthy body helps anybody think and perform better no matter the profession, but working out, eating, and sleeping only takes so long; other tasks needed to be accomplished to go from point A to point B.

Developing a rigid plan is something that's imperative to understand, and including the details is crucial to finding success in any endeavor, whether it's sports, business, or managing a family.

My family always joked that my dad had a plan that needed to be stuck to every vacation. But that joke eventually ran dry to me because I understood where he came from and that without a plan, you have no chance of organizing people, let alone leading them.

PERSISTENCE

Nothing will go according to plan. No, this isn't contradictory of the previous section. This is what ties the previous two together. A passion can be so strong for a certain sport or business; the plan may be thoroughly detailed down to every minute. Everything may look flawless on paper.

But then something goes wrong...

A goal isn't hit, a deadline is missed, or a game is lost. But how could that happen? My passion is there and my plan was detailed! Losses and failures occur for everyone, even the greatest. The Patriots in 2007 seemed pretty unstoppable with an undefeated season leading all the way to the Super Bowl. Things couldn't get better. Then all of a sudden, they lost. Even the public wondered how that was possible. Point being, is that there are unforeseen events that will occur, a surefire hit may flop, or what appeared to be a warm lead may have never been anything at all. But you counted on it! So what do you do next?

Learn and move on—persevere and grow. Perseverance is a trait all great leaders have. At some point you will lose, you will be doubted, and you may be the only one. It can feel close and lonely. But persevering will bring everything back. Identifying pieces of the plan that may have been wrong (and being humble enough to admit a mistake), then re-channeling the passion that got you started in the first place, will lead you back to where you want to go. The sting of a loss while doing something you're genuinely passionate about what will drive you to persevere and get it done the next time. Trust me; you won't want that feeling again!

THE POWER OF
FEARLESS
LEADERSHIP

> "I can accept failure.
> Everyone fails at something.
> What I can't accept is
> not trying."
>
> *Michael Jordan*

Basketball has always been my favorite sport to both watch and play. I know that sounds crazy coming from a former NFL player, but I wanted to play in the NBA so bad growing up. But then again, who didn't want to be "like Mike"? My favorite leaders who I looked up to and aspired to lead like were basketball players, most notably Michael Jordan. It was a great experience as a young athlete to witness his remarkable career, leadership moments, and championship accomplishments. Night in and night out, he laid it all on the line, took the risks, and sometimes failed, but he is remembered for the times he converted and had success.

ff When I think of fearless leadership, nobody comes to mind quicker than Michael Jordan. He didn't feel fear. INSTEAD, he embraced the challenge that lay ahead of him to bring his team back or close the game out. JJ

When called upon to make a game-winning shot in the iconic NBA finals against the Utah Jazz, he didn't fear missing. He knew that shot was going in, and he knew that he needed to lead his team back to victory. Many people remember that shot but forget his leadership throughout the game. For instance, on the possession before the big shot, Jordan came away with a clutch steal.

This would then lead to the opportunity for a game-winning shot. Most would feel defeat slowly creeping up and let the moment overcome them. But without the fear of failure, there wasn't a doubt of what the outcome would be in Jordan's mind.

A high level of leadership requires this level of fearlessness—genuinely believing that you can make it happen, even with your back against the ropes, against all odds, and when everyone has counted you out. There are far too many great athletic examples, but no competitor sticks out more to me and displays this trait better than Michael Jordan.

FEARLESS LEADERS DISTINGUISH FEAR FROM UNCERTAINTY

As a rookie, I feared the worst. I feared messing up the play, whether it was failing in a blocking assignment, running the wrong route, or just physically losing my match-up. My worries lived in the back of my mind and, ultimately, my performance suffered. I was wrapped up in myself. I had no chance to develop as a player or team leader because, each day, I was preoccupied with my individual performance and repercussions if it wasn't up to standard.

As a leader, you can't be afraid. You may not know what the outcome is going to be, but the fear of failing shouldn't drive you in the moment, but rather the excitement of the unknown and the euphoric feeling of achievement that ensues. Don't be afraid to put yourself out there in these moments and clutch situations. It's a time to shine or a time to learn, but definitely not a time to be afraid!

The first step in addressing fear is to distinguish fear from uncertainty. It's okay not to know what is going to happen, but there's no reason to fear the future. Many great leaders have pursued their goals without assurance that their plans would ever actually come to fruition. Adjusting your course will be something that happens as challenges come. Don't be alarmed by uncertainty.

> **❝Instead, welcome obstacles and challenges that will ultimately strengthen you**
> # AS A LEADER. ❞

Seeing that there is an unknown is perfectly fine—and, in fact, the reality of the unknown must be recognized—but there is no need to be afraid.

If people knew the exact outcome every single time, there would be no fun in the process and far less enjoyment once the challenge is complete. Embrace the moment and harness the excitement, not the fear.

FEARLESS LEADERS FOCUS ON WHAT THEY CAN CONTROL

As my second season in Miami approached, I began opening up about my fears. I started having conversations with other players on the team, many who were my peers in age and experience. We all had one big uncertainty on our minds—our job security.

We knew exactly what it looked like to lose a position without warning. We witnessed it daily: people were fired in the middle of meetings, just before practice, just after practice, at the start of the day, and at the end of the day. We'd show up at work and realize someone new was there and someone else was gone.

For a whole year, I had let the fear of being fired grow in my mind. Talking with my teammates, though, allowed me to realize that I wasn't alone. Some players dwelled on it constantly, obsessing over failing instead of thinking about success. Yet the guys I talked to who were older than me—guys who had been playing at a high level five, six, seven seasons or more, guys who had experienced the realities and pressures of professional sports—responded with great wisdom. According to these players, part of working towards success meant consciously choosing not to worry about losing a job. Whether or not they were fired on a particular day was something they didn't have much control over. They reminded me that where they did have control was in their performance at work, on the practice field, and in the meeting room. Whatever pertained to their assignment on a given day, that was what they could control, and that's what they chose to focus on. Regardless of how talented an individual was, a common theme was exerting maximum effort in every aspect of the game.

Of course, they were not immune to the fear of being fired. That thought has crossed every player's mind at some point, but the ones who had been around longest learned this was just the nature of the business.

ff Focusing on what you can control
your effort, attitude,
work ethic,
COMMITMENT,
will lead
TO SUCCESS.
Successful workouts, film sessions, practices, and, in turn, games, seasons, and
ultimately your career. 🗩🗩

The same principle applies for any area of leadership. Whatever your assignment or job, the only thing you can control is your effort. If you put your best out there, then you should be satisfied. You've done all you can.

The experiences and high-pressure nature of the NFL taught me how to embrace the unknown, but it's always a work in progress.

Transitioning out of football and into business, I learned that this same thought process existed but in a different format. I felt the fear of failing creeping back up. I was nervous to put myself out there because of what someone else may think, a review I may receive, or it just not working out well and everyone thinking I'd failed. But then I quickly realized none of that matters and it for damn sure doesn't help you succeed. If I'd failed in front of millions of viewers on national TV, why should I care about these little things in business?

Now you might be thinking, "Well, that doesn't help me because I didn't perform on a big stage previously." Wrong. It's only my example that helps me relax and get rid of any fear that may be lingering. Find a past example of when you put yourself out there and realize that this moment is no different. Realize that you have prepared, envisioned the success, and are ready for this moment. Be excited! Be confident!

FEARLESS LEADER SHARE CONFIDENCE IN THEMSELVES

Beginning that second season, after seeking out the advice of my colleagues, I realized that I couldn't be consumed by fear. I started to shift my perspective, and my confidence grew.

I found myself starting the third game in the pre-season and being utilized on my team in new ways. My coaches put me in a variety of roles, and I was given the chance to showcase my abilities with different positions on the field. I began to trust my training more—the hard work and skill that had gotten me to this level in the first place. I was on that field and in the game for a reason—because I belonged. And I started to believe this. It may sound stupid, but continuous, positive self-talk helped immensely. Why would I fear the worst when I had already achieved some of the best? I had done these blocking assignments many times before, both pass blocking and run blocking from different positions and against different defenses. Why continue to fear and think, What if I mess up?

> **❝ The best leaders
> have a large vision in sight
> and know the steps required to fullfill
> # THAT VISION
> and all the smaller goals and tasks
> along the way which need to be
> accomplished. ❞**

I started consciously visualizing what it would look like when I succeeded and did well—not in the big picture, but in each little play and each detail within a play. I asked myself, "What would the defense look like? What does the guy across from me look like and likely to do against this type of play? How did he approach a certain block?" After running the play through in my head the night before and the day of, I saw myself executing what I had practiced. I got my job done and showed that I could be relied upon when it counted.

The difference here was that I was acting and leading from a place of confidence. I'd visualized the success and had it before. Now on the big stage, it was simply trusting myself and replicating what I'd done countless times.

FEARLESS LEADERS TURN CONFIDENCE IN TO HARD WORK

Effective leaders cultivate an inner belief within themselves first, then pour that confidence into the rest of the group or organization. The step after that is to translate that confidence into hard work and diligence. My junior year at Kansas State, I was determined to win. I knew in my heart that we could be the best offense—not only in the Big Twelve, but also in the country. I knew that it would take an extensive amount of work to get there because we were competing against great talent from all across the country. Specifically in the Big Twelve, there were superstars on offense, such as Dez Bryant and Jeremy Maclin, who we'd be facing.

We worked hard that entire summer and all of off-season. There was one time when we stayed out late on the field—even when we weren't supposed to be there—doing extra routes and getting more running in. No one asked us to put in extra time, but we wanted to be the best and believed that we could be. We were willing to do whatever it took, even if that meant running routes in the summer heat when nobody was watching us or pushing us on. It's what you do when nobody's watching that defines a great leader. What you did in those moments comes to life when the spotlight is on. Not everyone wants to put in extra work, staying late, arriving early, or saying, "no" to a party or to a good time. Leading often means making decisions that aren't well liked.

❝What is RIGHT is not always popular. ❞

Sometimes people will critique not just individual decisions but your entire leadership style. Because you're putting yourself out there, people will watch you closely. Whether you're leading one person, yourself, a team of fifty, or a company of 10,000, people will notice you and examine your leadership. They will criticize and scrutinize. The best leaders, though, don't allow the criticism, scrutiny, and naysayers to deter them from their mission.

Don't be mistaken: Being a fearless leader does not mean that you won't ever fail. After my change of mentality in Miami—even with the same positive approach leading up to and during the game—I was taken down a couple of times against the Tampa Bay Buccaneers, the team I played with right out of college. It drew enough attention to warrant our head coach, Tony Sparano, asking me if I was trying to get myself cut—which is NFL language for fired.

Those weren't the words I wanted to hear after giving up a sack, but I didn't let fear cloud my mind. I knew what I would do moving forward to prove I deserved my spot on the team, and I focused on the future. The previous year, it would have been a different story. I would have allowed that fear to consume me.

My new perspective, gave me the ability to lead myself on the field, rebound from a negative play, and rattle off a series of positive ones.

❝ Losses are inevitable; bouncing back quickly and not dwelling on what's already happened is key to moving forward fast and FINDING SUCCESS. ❞

That second season in Miami proved to be a big jump for me. I played ten times the number of plays as the year before. I had my first reception and, ultimately, had substantially more fun and enjoyment than previous years. I was finally able to feel comfortable with what I was asked to do. Even if something had happened to a starter, or if I had been asked to step into a larger role, I could have done it because I wasn't leading from a place of fear. I was leading from confidence and trust. I was backing that confidence up with hard work on the practice field. I believed that I could step out on the field at any moment and do what I was asked to do.

I want you to think about how you're leading right now, whether you're leading yourself, a small group, a team, or a division within a large company. Are you leading from a place of fear? It's human nature to fear the unknown, but are you letting worry and doubt cloud your mind? Gain small wins, remain positive, trust your training and build toward your vision.

Takeaways:

1. Fearless leadership may not always be the most popular or well-liked decision.

2. Fearless leadership is developed during the times that nobody is watching.

3. Great leaders DO NOT fear an outcome, yet embrace the challenge that lies ahead.

STAND TALL
ARROGANCE VS.
HUMILITY IN
VICTORY
& DEFEAT

"Be a winner. Stand for something. Always have class, and be humble."

JOHN MADDEN

No, I didn't just call the book "Stand Tall" because I'm actually tall. I called it that because it is something I've struggled with my entire life. I've written and rewritten this chapter a number of times. It may be the most difficult to put down in writing, because it's possibly one of the most difficult aspects of leading and being in the limelight. It doesn't only apply to winning an NFL game in front of millions of people, then being on TV immediately afterwards discussing the game and choosing to praise the opponent or gloat at your accomplishments. Being in the limelight can be a one-on-one sales call or meeting with a prospect. It can also be what you decide to do with yourself when things don't go your way. It applies every single day.

" STANDING TALL
amidst a crushing loss,
and equally so during an
improbable victory,
is challenging every single time in
every moment. "

THE INNER COMPETITOR

Often times passion, mine included, is mistaken for arrogance. My passion for something also fuels my inner competitor to do whatever I can to win. Those who know me know this holds true for me in any sport, to business and even ping pong or cards games. I'm playing to win every time. This is something that I wish was easier to shut off, but I didn't pick up the paddle, the hand of cards, or begin the new business venture with the thought of losing. I'm always looking for a way to win.

The inner competitor in me started early. My mom loves to share a story with people of how intense and seriously I took a competition, even at a young age. I was born in the small town of Roseburg, Oregon, about three hours south of Portland. We lived at the end of the street surrounded by houses with other kids around mine and my siblings' age. We were always out playing some sort of game or sport in the street. Naturally, I wanted to be the best overall athlete on the block, and the time came to put an end to who was the fastest. The girl across the street ended up beating me in a race, and boy did everyone enjoy letting me hear about the loss. Feeling the sting of the loss and letting my emotions get the best of me, I immediately ran to my house and went straight for the hockey stick. Thankfully, my mom was watching the situation from the window and put a stop to me as soon as I entered the garage. She knew what just happened and how mad I was, but this was the first of many times she helped stop me, calm me down, and realize that it was just one loss...in a neighborhood foot race...at nine years old. It's pretty funny to think about now, but it reflects how seriously I take competition.

I'm always thankful to have had my mom there at my side while growing up to keep me corralled in times of defeat. Even before losing the foot race in the street, I was in a competition for who could read the most books in my first grade class. I wouldn't even speak to the other kids that were remotely close to beating me and let the others know how far ahead of them I was. My mom was also a teacher at the school, caught wind of this, and made sure I learned my lesson.

I could go on and on with examples and times when my mom was there in times of defeat to make sure I showed good sportsmanship and humility. She was also there with me when I won the ARA Sportsmanship Award after my senior year in college. The award was given to whomever best exemplified character, sportsmanship, and philanthropy, along with football excellence. I was honored to have received the award in front of a standing ovation at Bramlage Coliseum at Kansas State University, but even more honored to have received it in front of my mom.

Being able to regulate your competitive fire is an important ability to have. It isn't always easy, but it's what allows you stand tall during moments of defeat and remain humble in times of victory. In those tough times of a loss, learn from it (which we will discuss later), then move on from it and improve so that it doesn't happen again.

THANK THOSE IN YOUR CORNER

With any amount of success, someone was there to support you. There will be down times and there will be high times. I've always heard multiple times to not gloat, brag, or piss off the people you see or pass on your way up to the top, because they'll be the same people you come by when you trip up and stumble back down to the bottom.

"Standing tall during times of success is just as CRITICAL to being an impactful leader as it is during times of defeat."

Thank those who were in your corner or by your side.

This was an easy concept for me to grasp (far easier than remaining positive during times of defeat) because of my experiences in team sports, especially football. No matter the position I played while growing up, my success on the field was never due strictly to me. There were many teammates involved—coaches who put in hours to the game plan and support staff that made the whole operation possible so that I was able to perform at a high level. If you can't remain humble and thank those who helped you arrive to the top, then you were never meant to be there in the first place.

Takeaways:
1. Thank those that helped you get to where you are.

2. Appreciate support from people you may not even have spoken to.

3. Show appreciation for an opponent.

CHAPTER 3

CREATING
HIGH
PERFORMANCE
TEAMS

"When a team outgrows individual performance and learns team confidence, excellence becomes a reality."

Joe Paterno

What defines a high performance team? When thinking of high performance organizations, you might think of recently successful teams, the 2015 and 2016 Golden State Warriors, for instance. You may think of companies that consistently remain at the top of their industry, such as Nike or Apple.

But high performance teams don't only exist as Fortune 100 companies and professional sports teams. High performance teams and organizations exist at all age and skill levels. These teams know themselves well, they know thier own strengths and weaknesses, and intentionally develop their skills. They function as a unit, not individually. As a unit, these teams operate from a base of fast-twitch knowledge, which allows them to perform under pressure. It's easy to see when pressure mounts, or one link in the team is faced with a critical moment, to see just how strong the team is.

HIGH PERFORMANCE TEAMS KNOW THEIR WEAKNESSES AS A GROUP

The first step to creating a high performance team is identifying the weakest link in the team or the weakest parts of your system. In some cases, the weakest link could be an individual person or a group of people, such as one division or department. It could be a process or system—something that has to do with a service you deliver or your follow up with a new customer. If the team is an athletic team, it could be individual players, offensive or defensive schemes, or coaches. No one is above being the weakest link. This weakness could stem from the very top or the very bottom of the organization, but it needs to be identified—FAST! Without identifying the weakest link, you won't know what's missing in your process or what you're not doing well, and that leaves you susceptible to being blindsided.

After identifying the weakest link and figuring out what isn't working—what's consistently leading to a loss, a disconnect, a gap, a breakdown, or a bottleneck—it's time to decide how you're going to change (we'll discuss embracing change more in depth later).

When the weaknesses are stemming from certain individuals, those problems can be fixed in one of two ways. Either you train and develop the personnel already in place, or you look for new talent and different personnel outside the organization to bolster the team. I've always been a fan of developing the people who are already there, but I'm speaking from my perspective as a professional athlete who doesn't like to be replaced. I also think that someone may be ineffective because they're being taught or led incorrectly, and it's my job to fix it. Some organizations, though, may be looking for a solution within a pressing timeframe, so finding new people outside the organization to replace the weakest links may be the best option.

Even so, it's my opinion that, with great coaching and strong leadership, people can develop at a rapid rate. If you choose this route, it's important to figure out how to best communicate and teach who you're trying to train. Some people can handle a lecture, some people need to physically do something, and some may need pictures or diagrams. Sometimes it's a combination of the three.

ff Find out what
WORKS
and what doesn't. 🥚🥚

You cannot address these problems without first looking at the team as a whole to find what is going wrong. Don't get defensive if you ultimately find out YOU are the problem and need to change a leadership style or technique to better address the team.

HIGH PERFORMANCE TEAMS KNOW THEIR WEAKNESSES INDIVIDUALLY

In order to have a high performance team, not only do the weaknesses of the team need to be addressed, but every individual part needs to be functioning at its best. This is why you also have to look at yourself, individually, in the mirror to see where your breakdowns are and to discover where you are weak. Look at yourself and identify where you can be better.

If you're having trouble identifying where you're weak because you don't like admitting that you're bad at anything, which I know is true of some of us, ask the people around you. The people you report to, the people who report to you, your close friends, or your family may be able to help you see what isn't working well for you. Never be afraid of feedback and criticism.

After naming these weaknesses, figure out how you're going to solve them.

❝ Make a plan for what you can do on a micro level TO GET BETTER each day. ❞

For example, as an athlete, I understood at a young age that I wasn't the fastest kid on the team. At the same time, I knew that developing speed would help not only my individual performance but also the performance of the entire offense or defense. In turn, my speed would help my team and organization achieve our ultimate goal of winning a championship.

So my goal for myself was to be faster. But that wasn't a very specific goal, so I had to break that down into smaller tasks that I could accomplish on a daily basis to work towards my larger goal of getting faster. I added in a variety of speed and quickness drills all throughout my workouts during the week. Hip mobility, core strength, leg strength, explosiveness, range of motion, flexibility—all these were very small categories that I could improve in to increase my speed over time. By increasing my speed, I made myself a more versatile athlete and strengthened a current weakness in my game.

Some people, especially when looking at speed as an athlete, may feel that there is a ceiling to improvement: Once you reach a certain level, you can't go any further. This is something that a lot of elite athletes experience. It's called "diminished returns." Initially, as you put work into improvement, you will see rapid gains over days, weeks, or months. As time goes on, the rate of improvement slows down, and you might feel dejected.

This slowing is natural, and you can't let it bother you or drag you down. Continue to work on your weaknesses. Even when your weaknesses become strengths, continue to develop them. You may feel strong at your current level of play or competition, or you may feel strong in your role in your current organization, but as you are propelled further along in your career, as you reach more elite levels, you will again need to work on these areas. Becoming versatile and an asset in multiple ways also increases your overall value—this was the case for me in training camp my second year in the NFL. I could only get so fast, in a certain timeframe. I could definitely learn more positions to make me more valuable to my team

> ## "STRENGTHENING
> a personal weakness allows you to
> **propel yourself further**
> in your career and makes you
> a more **valuable** player. **"**

For me, working on my speed helped me move from high school football to college football. Once I got to college, I realized I needed to work on my speed again. If you review the Kansas State versus KU football film from 2006 and watch the first play of the game, you'll be able to see that I wasn't the fastest player on the field. However, I didn't let that stop me or define me on that team. I was able to work on my speed. I became faster and faster, and I wasn't as much of a liability for my team in the speed department.

HIGH PERFORMANCE TEAMS BUILD ON THEIR STRENGTHS

Identifying strengths is the next most important step to create a high performance team. Once you've identified the weak links of your processes or systems, on both corporate and individual levels, and made a plan to address them, turn to your strengths.

Look for what you do well as a team. What do people know you for? What do you use to define your organization? Look at the Golden State Warriors, and you'll recognize that they have outstanding three-point shooters, and those shooters have solid teammates to back up their game.

Having identified valuable strengths, never let those strengths weaken or turn into a problem for you. Spend time working on them. Neglect will slowly allow them to become weaknesses.

❝ Let your strengths become areas that you continue to **build** upon. ❞

Continuing with the example of the Warriors with their already-great three-point shooters, they added another weapon just as deadly as their current players with Kevin Durant.

My strength was always blocking. It was something that I did well, that I was known for, and that I could be counted on to do. Coaches at all levels, in high school, in college, then in the NFL, realized, "Hey, I can put him in here to make a block for us. Then we'll run the ball behind him to get first down or make a play if we need one." And, for the most part, I could perform.

I never let blocking turn into an area of weakness. I would always work on blocking in my training. Sometimes this meant doing very small drills working on blocking a nine technique. Sometimes this meant running a more complex drill, working on a combo block with a tackle or another tight end.

Continuing to work on your most valuable strengths, which for me was run blocking, is something that you can do on your own. Once again, break down the strength into smaller parts. What makes you great at it? Are you knowledgeable about what to do to implement it? Are you strong here individually, without the help of others? Do you have excellent technique? Knowledge, individual strength, and technique are all important in making a good run block.

The same principles apply to being a reliable part of a sales team, to being a team player in your division of the company, or to being a good leader in general. Know what it is that you need to do well and break down that activity into steps. Master each of these and practice master them consistently, even when no one is watching, so that you can be counted on to perform when it matters, when all eyes are on you.

HIGH PERFORMANCE TEAMS BUILD FAST-TWITCH KNOWLEDGE

Part of being prepared to perform is developing fast-twitch knowledge. What do I mean by fast-twitch knowledge? Growing up as an athlete, I knew about the importance of developing fast-twitch muscle fibers for fast reactions and quickness. A lot of sports involve fast-twitch moments of play where athletes have to react quickly to succeed. Having an intuitive sense of what to do and the ability to do it immediately, takes practice and much repetition— not simply just being quick.

Instant reactions are also important in the business world. How do you react when someone calls out of the blue, when you're unprepared for the call? Do you have fast-twitch knowledge to respond as needed? What if someone brings up a question related to business that isn't directly in your field but is still relevant to your field? Do you know how to react and what to say?

Knowing how to act in more than one position was a skill that became very important for me and is important to most football players. Tight end is a versatile position. You could be lined up next to the right tackle on one play, be a full back behind the guard on the next play, then be split out wide on another play. You could be in the slot later on in the game, or you could even be lined up in a running back position for pass blocking purposes. All of these different spots on the field require a different base of knowledge about what is happening. As a player, you can't be content to just know how to play one spot. You need to know the overall scheme of the game because, at a moment's notice, someone could get an injury, shuffling around the players and putting you in a new position.

This shuffling happens in business, too. If someone calls in sick, you may be asked to play a different role. If someone leaves, you may need to pick up the slack until a replacement is found. If a teammate isn't performing well, you may need to cover for that person. Don't just be focused on what fits nicely inside the boundaries of your specialty. Having fast-twitch knowledge for each part of the process will help make you valuable and stand out as an employee. Ultimately, your knowledge will build that high performance team that wins on a constant basis. This may also lead to the opportunity you're looking for to make the jump in your career.

The finest athletes in the world are able to operate in the fourth quarter and in overtime. They are able to make big plays to win games. The top CEOs out there faced with a challenge—a dip in sales, a missed revenue goal, or a decline in their stocks—are able to respond with brilliant ideas to please the shareholders. Reacting with precision and performing under pressure are required of a successful, high performance teams, and these traits come through practice and development.

You have to work hard every day to build a consistently successful team. Identifying your weakest links, building upon your strengths, and developing fast-twitch knowledge are fundamentals of creating a high performance team.

Takeaways:

1. Identify your individual weaknesses, personnel weaknesses, and process weaknesses. From there, create a plan to develop them into strengths.

2. Never neglect your strengths and what you're known for. Take time to keep these aspects or traits strong.

3. Develop fast-twitch knowledge— the ability to think and react with precision and accuracy at a moment's notice under high pressure.

CHAPTER 4

GAIN
CONTROL
BY LETTING GO

"Good teams become
great ones when the
members trust each other
enough to surrender the
'me' for the 'we.'"

Phil Jackson

Everyone strives to have control in some area of life. For some, it's control of a circumstance or situation. For others, it's a certain relationship. Or sometimes people look to control a group, team, or organization. Whatever area of your life needs attention, know that control comes through preparation, confidence, but most importantly, through letting go.

CONTROL BEGINS WITH RECOGNIZING LIMITS

What I found most nerve wracking when starting off in the NFL was the severe lack of job stability. Many don't view an NFL position as an actual job, but that is what it is. Your employers are organizations like the Miami Dolphins, and they are paying you in the same way that you would be paid by Nike or Columbia Sportswear—so technically, it's a job.

With an NFL position, however, the threat of losing your job is particularly high. Daily, I witnessed people getting fired. The organization consistently brought in new people—brought them right in front of you—to test them out and compare them with current players. You definitely never had the chance to feel complacent. You knew your employers were always looking to see if there was someone better out there to replace you. Like any good organization, they kept you working hard for your spot on the team.

It was a stressful situation. The thought of being fired lodged itself in my head and affected my performance. I kept wanting to have control over my employment, and that obsession influenced the way I felt and performed each day. When my mental focus was not on the task directly in front of me, I was compromised—not just physically, but emotionally and mentally as well. When a task required my best attention, I was distracted and not able to execute.

So after talking with some of the older players and my peers on the team, I began to understand that I wasn't the only one who felt like this. Many players felt the pressure of keeping their job at some point in their career. So, moving into my second year, I made a change. I decided to let go. I had always feared something I couldn't control. I could not control who was hired and who was let go. What my team decided to do would happen no matter what I did. So I stopped trying to control it.

I saw this simple change catapult me forward that year as my play improved and my productivity on the field increased.

ff Recognizing what you can and cannot **control** will make a **significant impact** on your overall **PERFORMANCE. ,,**

CONTROL COMES THROUGH PREPARATION

What I could control was my own attitude, effort, drive, and, most importantly, preparation. I took preparation very seriously. I knew that being able to understand all aspects of the game—everything going on around me—would make me more valuable. I studied different positions, their assignments and unique situations, so I could understand not just the tight end position, but also the responsibilities and experiences of the tackle, the guard, the center, the receivers, the quarterback, the running backs—everyone. Studying each part of the larger play helped me be better prepared to do my piece.

❝ Through preparation came confidence. ❞

When I stepped on the field and heard the play, I didn't have to think hard about what I needed to do. My role in the play instantly came to mind. I had prepared, and I was ready to go. All of the pieces were there. My confidence was there because I knew my role. I had prepared on the practice field. I knew what the other team was most likely going to run, so I knew what to expect. With each of these pieces in place, the game seemed to slow down, and I began gaining control of the situation—but I would never have gained this control if I didn't finally let go of things that were holding me back.

CONTROL COMES THROUGH PREPARATION

My dad was our high school's head football coach. We were living in Beaverton, a suburb of Portland, and he was at a new high school. Before this move, my dad had coached in rural southern Oregon. At first, he brought the blue-collar, hard-nosed approach that he had used in those programs to this new school. However, micromanaging every coach and player, trying to keep a firm control on everyone, did not work for this program.

When I entered high school, I started playing for his team and, living in the same house as him, I was able to advocate for the team and say, "Hey, you can trust us to get our job done. You can trust us to know that we know what we're doing." His yelling, aimed at each person for every individual slip-up, was not really helping our team or our play.

My dad began to let out the reins he had on the team and allowed the coaches to coach their individual players and let players lead each other. The whole organization began to run more organically and efficiently. Everything was based on the overall values that he, as head coach, had instilled in the program, but he didn't drill them home on us every day. This step back actually provided him with more control of the team and ultimately more freedom.

My dad isn't just any coach—he was coach of the year in the state of Oregon in both football and track. He is a man who has coached multiple all-star games and many athletes who earned division one scholarships. Much of his success has stemmed from letting go a little bit, easing off micromanaging, and trusting in the organization and its processes.

Granted, my high school team didn't end up winning a championship, but the year after I graduated, they finished runner-up; then three years later, they won a title with my younger brother on the team. My dad has since thanked us for talking him into losing his grip on the team. He recognizes this change as one of the better decisions he has made as a coach.

Certainly, you need to instill leadership and values into the group you are leading, but hanging over people's heads and micromanaging is not the best way to help your group to succeed or move forward quickly. Letting people grow and learn from their mistakes is extremely helpful. When they fix their own mistakes, they can learn and move forward again, this time faster. Your team won't get to this place, though, until you realize that you need to let go of some of that fear of making mistakes. Allow yourself to gain control by having confidence in your team. They'll ultimately be more responsive to you.

CONTROL COMES THROUGH LETTING GO OF FEAR

Resistance to the idea of letting go stems from fear of loss. Don't worry about what you may lose because then you probably will lose it. It is clear to see how fear interferes with performance. Time and time again, with any level of athletics, you can watch a team who gains a lead stop playing to win and begin playing not to lose. Even when ahead in the game, the leading team will lose with a comeback by the underdog. People say, "Well, that's because they're playing not to lose." The team is afraid of losing.

People worry, "If I begin to let go, does that mean I'm losing control or that I'm undisciplined? Does it mean that I'm scattered"?

No, it doesn't. When you eliminate the fear of losing control, you begin to gain control.

Fear of loss isn't what fuels a team. Spending time worrying about what you can't control isn't time well spent. You're not helping yourself or changing anything. Instead, you can find energy and control in accomplishing your goals—especially personal goals. Don't worry about extraordinary circumstances that are unlikely to happen, and let go of circumstances that you cannot control. Stick to your plan for success, following it day in and day out. Focus on what you can control—which can be anything from regulating your diet to adjusting your sleeping habits. Your daily habits and decisions are within your sphere of control. Focus on those minor things that you choose to do throughout the day that will ultimately lead to your success.

Takeaways:

1. Let go of the fear of failure and things out of your control. Direct that energy towards things you can control, like your effort.

2. Preparation is the best way to feel in control. Understand more than just your role, work towards understanding

GAME ON! THE
WELL-OILED
MACHINE

> "It's not the will to win that matters. It's the will to prepare to win that matters."
>
> *Paul "Bear" Bryant*

A well-oiled machine is finely tuned, lubricated, and ready to go. It does not break down. There is no rust. It's working perfectly. In the world of sports, this image of a machine is used to describe a team, offense, or defense that is working well together. Everyone on the team is clicking, and they are successful as a group. People say that the group is firing on all cylinders.

How can you create a well-oiled machine in the team that you lead? How do you get to that point of being able to move, as a group, at light speed, making rapid decisions left and right and continuing to press forward no matter what? What led to this development? How do you have that efficiency within your organization, team, division, or group?

A WELL-OILED MACHINE KNOWS THEIR OPPOSITION

What a lot of people do not realize or appreciate about football is the amount of calculation and thought behind every single play. There's an immense amount of preparation that goes into the game every Sunday. It isn't just a free-for-all. It's like a game of chess.

Before a game, an NFL team has a week of preparation. On Wednesdays, we focused just on the first and second down and what blitzes the opposing defense likes to use in these situations. How were we going to attack the team on these two downs? What types of blitzes did they use in these situations? Did they even have a favorite one or two, or did they devise a new blitz each week? We had to figure out how we were going to attack the team that was strategizing to defend against us—starting with where the majority of the game takes place—between the twenty yard lines and on first and second down.

This was where we would get the machine rolling each drive. We looked at whomever we were facing that week: Who were their personnel? Who were their playmakers? We started with that. What did we know about them—their size, speed, and tendencies? What did they like to do? What should I look for? How much could I find out about the people on the other side of the ball?

After finding out as much as possible about the personnel, the next step was to look at the tendencies of the team as a whole. What were the kind of plays they liked to make? Did they like to bring a blitz on first down? Did they like to bring pressure on second down? Did the second down blitz depend on if you gained yards on the first down? If so, how many yards?

You can pick up on a team's tendencies and get tips about what they might do by studying film from past games. Typically, this is done throughout the week. What many football fans do not realize is that—with the exception of an injured player who might take extensive time in the treatment room—the combined time, on average, a player spends on the practice field, in the weight room, and in the treatment room, is much less than the amount of time a player spends in the meeting room and watching film. Football games are very calculated and organized, and each play is made with precision and a lot of attention.

So, on Wednesday, we focused on first and second down. We got an understanding of their base personnel—who their key players were, who we were going to see on first and second down, and what their tendencies were (did they like to blitz from the strong side, the weak side, or up the middle, etc.)? After this, we would then go practice our plan of attack against a simulated defense to get a feel for how our plan would come together on Sunday. Then Thursday we would move into third down and go over what the opposing defense liked to do in these situations. Friday was red zone, short yardage, and goal line scenarios, and Saturday would be a final walk-through. Each day built upon the last to put together a full plan of attack for Sunday.

The point is that every organization has tendencies and patterns that you may be able to predict based on their personnel. Maybe they have a CEO that's very forward thinking and doesn't want a rusty old idea. Maybe there is someone in leadership who doesn't like new processes and is scared of change. In this case, you may need to ease into pitching an idea a little bit differently than you would with a more progressive thinker.

Everybody is unique. Never treat one organization or one team the same as another or assume a deal from one company to the next is going to be just like the previous one. Everybody's needs are different. Everybody's way of operating is different. Everybody comes from a different culture. Everybody's personnel are different. So prepare for each situation individually. Spend time studying the situation that you are going to be facing, and study who is involved. You have to know who you are up against.

A WELL-OILED MACHINE HAS A UNIFIED VISION

Obviously the goal and vision is to win. Nobody is doing something to lose. But how would a win be accomplished? It doesn't just happen randomly, especially not at an elite level in a pressure-filled environment. There is always preparation that you can do ahead of time to build a plan, gain an advantage, and create a well-oiled machine. I know I just talked about what we assess about our opponent each day of the week leading up to the game, but how did that translate to what were we going to do? What kinds of running plays were we going to have? What kinds of passing plays were we going to have? How could we best attack this as a group to get a win?

After meeting as the entire offense, we split up into smaller groups. For example, the quarterbacks and receivers might go one direction to discuss the passing game, while the rest of the offense, the running backs, linemen, and tight ends got together to discuss the running game, breaking down their responsibilities and how each piece would come together to create success.

We started with the macro level of what the team was going to do to attack on offense, and then that plan was broken down into parts from a running standpoint; finally, we took the plan down one last level to division by position. What were we, as just the tight ends, going to do, either one-on-one or two-on-two? How would we position ourselves when there were multiple tight ends on the field? If there was only one tight end in the game, which one of us was in? Sometimes it was one guy the whole time. Sometimes we brought in a different person for this specific assignment because he was better at handling a certain kind of situation. The same communication can work for any organization. You have to approach the company or division as a whole so that everyone is on the same page about your end goal. If people do not understand the vision, how can they work towards it?

Then, to make the best use of everyone's time, break the strategy down into segments so each part can work together on their respective tasks. Collaboration within divisions is especially helpful to get more people on the same page faster. Why not institute collaboration more often to ensure that people are working well together? When people are more familiar with each other, they can produce a better outcome as a unified group rather than when they work as independent segments of the team.

THE WELL-OILED MACHINE DRIVES HOME POINTS

After addressing first and second down, getting everyone on the same page, and breaking up into groups on Wednesday, Thursday strictly focused on third down, following the same procedures. On Friday, we moved forward to talk about the red zone.

Friday was the finale. First and second down moved us down the field. Maybe we had some stops or we got stopped in our first game plan, so our next game plan during third down was ready to move us forward—to keep moving the chains. Finally, we were ending in the red zone. We had the opportunity to score points. What were we going to do here? This—the red zone—was where we really needed to convert. How were we going to get in there and put the ball in so we gained points and won the game?

As our coaches always reiterated, there was a lot of timing and precision in this final piece. Everything tightened up here. The windows were small. There was no chance of the defense getting beat over the top because the field ends, so the details became even more important here. The timing was critical and had to be superior—even more so than in the field.

The same preparation process applies in the world of business. Wednesday handles the initiation: how are we going to initiate the game plan, the attack? How are going to initiate the sale? Thursday is the third down day—how are we going to handle objections and obstacles that may come up? What if our first plan gets stopped—what are we going to go do next? That's the second day.

The last day is about driving home the points. We're in the position we wanted to be in. We're in the driver's seat or we're in crunch time with negotiations—we need to make the offer, we need to make the advancement. What does that look like? How do we do that? How do we make that happen? What's the exact language we need to use? Maybe one word is more powerful than another, or maybe a word should be moved here or there. Maybe the emphasis should be on a different point or a different part of the sentence. Seemingly small details can make all of the difference in moving the ball forward and getting the points, getting the goal, getting the touchdown, or achieving whatever end result you want.

The plan has been broken down, day to day, group to group, so that everyone knows what the strategy is, down to the smallest division. Every last individual has an understanding of their specific group's goal, the larger division's goal, and the overall team goal.

When the process and preparation is done well, each team member can say, "Hey, I know that I know the plan, how we do business, and how we will get things done come Sunday, the money day. We're a well-oiled machine."

A WELL-OILED MACHINE UTILIZES THE "WHAT IF" WALK THROUGH

Some of you, however, may be dealing with a particularly difficult situation. Perhaps you are encountering some hesitation from your clients. Maybe you're dealing with a real wild card—you have to face a person or an organization that seems completely unpredictable. You might not know what they're going to throw at you.

When I was playing for the Dolphins, as well as the Raiders, we did something every Friday called the "what if" walkthrough. I always liked it and found it valuable.

What was the "what if" walkthrough? It's pretty simple. We'd gone through our opposing team's tendencies and what they're likely to do in every different scenario and area of the field. We'd seen what they've been showing week in and week out. Our game plan was detailed and well researched. Come Friday, just before practice that day, we walked through the "what ifs" of what else they might do. We brought up different reactions and options—we tried moving people around. Then we imagined that someone had an injury and needed to be replaced. Who would execute their work on the field? Who would step in? In the corporate world, sometimes people need to be replaced. What if someone is sick on the day of the big meeting or the big sale—is someone ready to fill those shoes?

The "what if" walkthroughs allowed an opportunity to discuss what to do if something unusual happened. When we were prepared for the unusual, we were able make more conversions happen. We were able to increase our fast-twitch knowledge so that we could immediately respond to every situation. Players could go out to make plays and not be worried about thinking, "Well, what do I do now?" They were ready for all situations and anything that came up.

Work a "what if walkthrough" into your organization's rhythm so that everybody within that team or group is prepared, not just the base situations and expected scenarios, but the

Takeaways:

1. A well-oiled machine knows their opposition, inside and out, and is ready for any unexpected situations.

2. Prepare for the unexpected with a "what-if walkthrough."

3. Make sure the big vision is understood by all and then break down how each person fits into the equation to reach that vision or end goal.

CHAPTER 6

VISUALIZATION
READING THE FIELD

Champions aren't made in the gym. Champions are made from something they have deep inside them—a desire, a dream, and vision."

Muhammad Ali

People talk about keeping the big picture in sight time and time again. They say that you need to see the overall goal, keep in mind the larger vision, look for the light at the end of the tunnel, imagine the end result, or picture success.

But what a lot of people aren't clear on is paying explicit attention to the details which helps you achieve that goal or assists in getting to the light at the end of the tunnel. The details are what, throughout the process, create the small wins. And the small wins build momentum that lead to the big goal at the end.

SUCCESS IS IN THE DETAILS

Sure, sometimes the big picture needs to be revisited. Depending on the situation, perhaps you review it daily, weekly, monthly, quarterly, or yearly. An end goal is important—whether it's a twenty-five year projection of a company or a one-year goal of a team, it requires attention.

But what a lot of people aren't clear on is paying explicit attention to the details which helps you achieve that goal or assists in getting to the light at the end of the tunnel.

SUCCESS COMES THROUGH VISUALIZATION

Detailing out every part of your plan means imagining what's ahead. What does each step look like? What does each day look like? What does each hour look like? When it comes time for the big sale or the big presentation, have you visualized the event going well? What the room looks like? What it smells like?

For me, visualization was something that significantly helped my overall performance. I started, in small ways, doing it naturally in high school, but I really learned the importance of it in college and in the pros. I learned how including more and more detail allowed me to feel more comfortable, in control ,and prepared—because I'd been there before mentally.

In high school, I remember, the night before a game, I would run plays over and over in my head. I'm sure many athletes have experienced that sort of visualization before a game, imagining the plays going positively or negatively, going one way or another. I would go through each play, picturing what could possibly happen, replaying in my mind what the first play of the game was going to look like. Usually, we knew what that first play was going to be, and we had studied the defensive tendency of the opposing team. How could I imagine myself responding? What were the other possibilities I needed to be prepared for (the what-ifs)?

When I was playing quarterback in high school, I envisioned the first play and every single option that could possibly be available to me—where I could throw if it was a passing play or where I would run if it was a running play. What if I needed to make an adjustment based on the certain shift by the defense? I wanted to know my options inside and out and have straightened out all the wrinkles in the game plan, before I even stepped on the field.

But those are the intellectual details of the game—details that had already been ingrained in my mind by the coaches. But the intellectual parts of the game were not the entire picture. When I was in college, one of our guest speakers before a game told us about how he utilized the power of visualization to prepare. He instructed us, "Don't just visualize the play and what you're going to do in the play. Granted, that is what's right in front of you, and, of course, that's what's most important. You can't succeed without knowing your role. After you know your role, though, be sure to visualize the score of the game, the wind, the weather, the daylight, stadium, the field, and the sounds of the crowd."

Imagine what each of your senses are telling you. Give circumstantial detail to the visualizations: Is it the first play of game or the second quarter or the third quarter? Are you coming off another previous play that did well? Are you coming off from a play that went poorly? Is momentum on your side, in your favor? Is it against you? Visualizing these environmental details in addition to the details of the play, for me, made a big difference.

SUCCESS COMES THROUGH MAKING ADJUSTMENTS

Of course, what happens isn't always what was visualized, and

This happens all the time in football, business, and life. There are many different factors that can cause unexpected changes, but how are you going to respond?

When I would envision the game the night before, I sometimes saw situations unraveling, and I realized that we could be coming to any particular play from various situations. We could be coming to this play running on momentum—right on the heels of a great play. But then again, maybe the previous play did not work out. We might need to change our plans and go to another play. How do we respond to that play? What may happen if things don't go right? How am I going to respond?

So I visualized success and how I planned to build upon that success, but I also visualized the possibility of a play not going well and what the response could be.

> ❝ It is important that we all
> # BE REALISTIC:
> Not everything is going
> to go **your way** all the time. ❞

If that were the case, you'd see more football games with scores of 100 to 0, undefeated seasons, and business empires that never experienced a decline in sales.

Sometimes you may need to step up in a way that you didn't plan on. Being in the practice of visualization, throughout every day, will help you here. You've visualized what to do, and this visualization will help you in any unexpected situation.

Having practiced many different strategies also helps. There were a lot of plays that we would practice in the off-season in

OTAs (Organized Team Activities, what the NFL calls Spring Training) or in spring football for college. We might not revisit those plays until training camp in August. Then, come week one, when playing a certain opponent, we chose to go with the game plan that called for a certain portion, say 40 percent of what we'd covered in both the spring and in August. Then, all of a sudden, something happened in that game. We'd only planned on using 40 percent of what we've learned, but now maybe we needed to draw from our larger knowledge base, using perhaps 10 percent more of what we knew to make a sudden change.

Certainly, preparing by visualizing the specific role that has been given to me is something I can do and be ready for. It's what's asked of me. But your team can make bigger jumps and see bigger success if each player is able to visualize what to do if the play does not go as planned. What if something comes up? What if you have to make this change? What if you need to bring in some of your other knowledge—perhaps 10 percent, 15 percent, 20 percent, or 30 percent of what is in your arsenal? You may not have necessarily prepared for using these skills that week, but you've learned them and practiced them at other points in your career.

I visualized these situations day in and day out. Maybe I didn't visualize a particular play versus this particular opponent or in this particular situation, but I visualized it happening in some situation. So even though the situation was unexpected, it wasn't the first time I was facing it. I had addressed it before. I'd seen the situation play through my head, and my mind could relax instead of racing with the anxiety of a new situation. I was able to operate calmly and smoothly. I was able to handle situations that might cause panic in others.

SUCCESS COMES THROUGH CLARITY

Bringing this full circle, before the night of the game, we were given the first ten plays, at least, that were going to be called offensively. And as I mentioned, we knew what the tendencies of the other team were. So when we got the ball, we knew how this team played—not just in general, but even what they were like at home compared to on the road and what they do against a team with this style of offense instead of against one with a different style. There were a lot of variables, but I knew what we were planning on doing and what to expect.

I also knew, though, that I could make an adjustment should something go wrong. I knew the overall rules that I learned in the spring and in August. I also had confidence that, in general, I'd studied their style, their distinct characteristics, as well as their second and third options. I was ready to go, and I knew what to visualize. I knew what I was going to be up against out there on the field, I knew what I was going to do to have success individually, and I knew what my teammates were going to do to succeed.

At the level of the NFL, you can also look ahead to see the forecast of the game, a report which reveals who the referees for the game will be. This might seem like a minor factor not relevant to every play, but who the referees are becomes crucial if you know that a certain referee often calls a certain penalty. Perhaps this referee tends to call illegal formation due to lining up off the ball. If you're trying to get a little bit of an advantage in pass protection, this will be important information. Maybe the referee is likely to call an illegal shift if you're not set. When it comes to simple penalties like that, having an awareness of the referee can only help you in your success in that game.

Also, if you make these mistakes, having known in advance that the referee was likely to call them, then you look like the dumb one.

The same goes for the weather. Check the weather forecast. You may need a different pair of cleats or different clothing to keep you warm. Since the weather is discussed beforehand, you know what you need to visualize and mentally prepare for. If it's going to be cold, start telling yourself, " it might be a little cold, so dress appropriately and be prepared for it."

Now, I've already visualized my responsibilities and the team's tendencies. I've imagined where the play is going to go, so now when it comes time to run the play, I've visualized all possibilities and all aspects of what's going on. Now I can strike properly and succeed. I can play even faster because I'm calm and relaxed mentally.

I've applied this same detailed vision to my own business, and it has been successful there as well. Imagine the situation you are going into. For people in sales, maybe you have a meeting to make a one-on-one sale. You could be a car salesman, and you've got customers coming in. You know the people, and you know what they look like. You can walk through in your head what the conversation may be like, what they may be interested in. You can go through what you think they may need and what they might go for, and you have a few options lined up for them.

And you can visualize more than just the conversation. Visualize what happens as the sale is made—all the way to the final swipe of the credit card or to the submission of the down payment. Or, even further in the future, imagine the success or enjoyment that family may have in that car—the experiences and vacations they may have. Visualize the entire process through to the end. You've heard about how runners run a race: they don't just stop right at the finish line, they run through the finish line. So why should you let your mind stop right at the finish line when visualizing? Let your mind run through the finish and see where that may lead to, what it may snowball into. Maybe your vision is so detailed and unique that it captivates your clients, who might send someone they know in to work with you because they enjoyed such a smooth experience with you.

You've taken a process—a sale or a presentation—that, normally, people are afraid of, and you've turned it into more business. Perhaps you're a speaker or you represent your company around the country and have to make different pitches. Ask yourself some questions: What does the boardroom look like? Who's in the room? What are they like? What might their questions be, their concerns, their complaints? What are all the questions I can ask? What experiences have I had in the past that might inform this meeting? What surprises have I had in the past? What will it look like for them to sign the deal? What's the color of the paper? What's the style of the pen? What's the signature look like? What's the color of the table, the color of the room, the lighting outside? All of these details need to be pictured and visualized in your head so that when you're in the situation, it slows down. You become very present. You become aware as if it has already happened before—even though it hasn't—and that's where you'll find the most success.

Execute fearlessly and move forward. Learn from mistakes. Continue to visualize situations and build upon those visualizations. I know my process of visualization has developed since high school. I've been working on it for about thirteen years, but I'm continuing to grow and master this skill. The more practice you have, the more clarity you'll have. Through visualization, I'm seeing the possibilities for my future.

Takeaways:

1. Once prepared for the task at hand and you have all the information needed, utilize visualization to help walk yourself through the upcoming situation mentally.

2. Visualization will allow for increased performance, a sense of more control, and relaxation.

3. It's never perfect, so be ready for something to go wrong and have more than one answer to respond with.

CHAPTER 7

GETTING T-BONED
WHEN A LOSS IS A
WIN

"Losing doesn't make me want to quit. It makes me want to fight that much harder."

PAUL "BEAR" BRYANT

When a loss is a win: It sounds counterintuitive, but it's the truth. Losing is part of the process of every aspect of life. The question is not how to avoid losing, but rather how will you utilize the experience gained from those losses (because they're going to happen). After each loss, whether it's minor or massive, you need to evaluate what did and didn't work, dissect what led to the loss, and then go build upon the new findings to make sure it doesn't happen again. Don't dwell on it, move on from it, and go create more wins.

LOSING BUILDS CHARACTER

Throughout my Little League Baseball career, I thought I was destined to be the next Randy Johnson or Ken Griffey Jr. I was a lefty, so nothing looked better to me than Ken Griffey Jr.'s sweet lefty swing, and since I was always a tall kid—a big kid on the mound and bigger than most of the kids that I played against—I always liked Randy Johnson because of his nickname, the Big Unit. There were multiple times when parents from the opposing team approached my mom to ask for a birth certificate to make sure I was in the appropriate age bracket—a ridiculous request.

But the lessons I learned from Little League Baseball honestly carried me throughout the rest of my life. When I was nine years old, ten years old, eleven years old, and twelve years old, my coaches told me that our Little League team was the best in our district. Every single one of those years, I worked my butt off in the summer to be a great pitcher, to be a top-notch first baseman, and to be able to hit the ball consistently when at bat. Every single one of those years, we lost in the championship.

As a nine-year-old, when we lost, it was my first time trying. I figured, "Hey, I'm going to make it back to the championship. Next year, as ten-year-olds, we'll be the older kids in the nine and ten division, and we'll be able to win this." The next year, though, the same thing happened. We lost to the same team. As an eleven-year-old, the same cycle came around. I thought we had a great team. Then we beat the team that had beat us in the first round, only to end up losing to them twice in the championship. We had, again, failed to make it out of district-level play.

As a twelve-year-old, my family moved up to the Portland Metro area, and I was part of one of the premier Little League teams in the area. This team routinely won not only in the district, but also in the state. Their players had gone on to make marks in the western Little League region in San Bernardino. My cousins actually helped start the program and brought it to prominence. I was excited to join the team to help continue that early success. We figured that it was only natural that we would steamroll everybody in Oregon on our way down to California. We planned, ultimately, to go on to Willamsport and play in the Little League World Series, which had always been a dream of mine.

After making it through the tournament with ease, we waited on the championship game to see who won from the loser's bracket. We were in a position where we had to lose twice to disqualify from the next round. Sure enough, it happened again. We lost two times, even as the favorites.

It had been four years of losing the same tournament over and over to the same team. Every single time, my mom would approach me after the game. She knew how important these games were to me. She knew how much I hated losing in general—especially to the same people, especially when my team was considered the better team and when we had been pegged as the favorite. It felt unfair. She helped me handle the situation. She always said, "Losing will help you build more character," and I always wanted to respond by screaming, "What good does that do me now? I lost the game. I feel like crap. The whole summer was for nothing." I wanted to move on and get to the World Series. I was crushed.

It sounds silly to share a story from childhood athletics when I have countless, more prominent examples from my collegiate and professional career. But there are two things that crossed my mind when deciding on the most pertinent example to share. One of them is a question I routinely get, especially now working with high school athletes, and that is, "What's something my child can do to be successful?" Learning to deal with failure, responding and growing from it, has been one of the most valuable lessons I learned through athletics and is something that has to happen to have success. Failure is inevitable and a loss is coming. How will you respond when it strikes?

The second question I am often asked is, "When did you decide you were going to play professional football?" I don't have an exact answer on that, but probably around my sophomore year in high school is when football came into the picture and the future looked promising. But that question relates to the example of building character through Little League baseball. The habits that helped me find success were developed and built upon at an early age. I practiced them unknowingly year in and year out, going from season to season, creating more experiences and learning opportunities to build from.

Looking back at my time in Little League, I can see how those words grew to become meaningful to me as I moved on to my high school, college, and professional careers. Everybody knows that, to kids, what's important to you is what's right in front of you. My mother's wisdom continued to help me when my present situations felt overwhelmingly important. Losing that tournament over and over and over and over helped build the character the I could rely upon throughout my coming professional years. My character was able to keep me strong and help me deal with adversity when circumstances got tough or didn't go my way—something that routinely happened again and again.

SUCCESSFUL PEOPLE LOSE

I realize, though, my story is not unique or unusual. This kind of repeated disappointment could happen to anyone. Think of the most successful people you've heard of. It may appear on the surface level that everything goes right for them all the time. But they've dealt with something tough. They've dealt with a piece of adversity. They've been down in the ditch—in a really bad place mentally, physically, and/or emotionally—and had to overcome an obstacle that seemed insurmountable.

Like I said, nobody likes losing. Losing just makes you feel infuriated. You feel terrible; you're emotionally down. You wonder why you even put yourself in that situation in the first place—a situation where you want to win with everything inside of you, but you end up just watching someone else celebrate right in front of you.

But the idea that successful people have only experienced success—that idea is completely untrue. Know that no one is exempt from losing at some point in their life. You are going to be blindsided at various times. Certainly, you can and should do all you can to look ahead, to see what's coming around the corner, and to find out what's around the corner after that one. But even if you look ten years ahead and plan everything out, there's always going to be something that comes through that was unforeseeable, that was unaccounted for. You need to be able to adjust—to learn the lesson and grow. Don't beat yourself up about it, because just like everyone breathes the same air, everyone deals with loss. How will you respond?

CHALLENGES REQUIRE CONTINUOUS DEDICATION

Certainly people experience challenges when working towards a goal. Even reaching success, however, is not an escape from adversity or failure. It is impossible for you to stay at the top forever, no matter what field you are in. Whether you're number one in the Fortune 500, whether you're number one in the NFL, whether you're number one quarterback in the league, or even if you're the best athlete in the world, you cannot remain number one forever. Eventually, someone else—another team or division—rises up and contests your position. There's always going to be someone else working for what you have.

I learned this lesson when I made it to the NFL. I never will understand why people celebrate after getting drafted. Well, I understand part of it. Everyone is proud when a player gets drafted to a team, and it's definitely an exciting time, but they're wrong to think that his dreams and goals have finally been achieved. Once you get drafted, you still need to make the cut for the final fifty-three-man roster...and then prove you belong every single day. You won't find out if you made it until the last day of training camp at the end of August, before the first game. So while everyone is congratulating players for being drafted—and, sure, it's an accomplishment—it's not a distinction that translates to making the cut. You still have to prove yourself on the field in order to make the team.

When I didn't get drafted after college, it felt like a big loss. I wondered what happened. I thought I had done well. I was a first-team, all Big Twelve tight end. I helped set records at Kansas State, and then things didn't go well for me with the draft. They picked 255 players, and I wasn't one of them. Out of all the football players in the country, I wasn't one of the best 255. I was disappointed, and I was mad.

Even so, I had dealt with challenges before in my life, so I kept on pushing.

The challenges kept coming. I signed as an undrafted free agent to the Tampa Bay Buccaneers. I went to OTAs, rookie minicamp, and training camp—where I was eventually cut. I took a quick trip to the New England Patriots and was in the room with Rob Gronkowski and Aaron Hernandez for a day and a half before getting cut...again. Finally, I made it to Miami where I would remain for three years.

They assigned me to the practice squad, which was eight players outside of the fifty-three—a group of the next people that they thought could contribute to the team of people that they wanted to develop. So I started off week one and two on the practice squad and then, eventually, made it on the fifty-three-man roster.

So all those challenges—not getting drafted, not making it in training camp with Tampa Bay, not being able to stay in

New England—eventually led to my spot here on the practice squad in Miami, which was a success. It was better than being at home, not having a job, and being out of football, but it still wasn't what I wanted. Having dealt with those earlier losses as a kid—not just with Little League Baseball, but with multiple other situations—helped me deal with these losses later in my life, and, ultimately, helped me push through until I made progress towards my goals.

Sure, I felt terrible for getting cut. Being called into an office to have somebody tell me, "You're not quite good enough," feels like shit. It's hard to hear that you did not make it, but hearing this at a young age, dealing with failure and adversity ever since I was a kid, helped me deal with challenges again when I was older. I know twenty-one is, in many people's perspective, still young—and it is—but it was an age when I was at a critical point in my football career. I needed to be able to look at myself. I saw where my blinders were and where I needed to develop to prove that I could play at this level. I was able to hear what other people said wasn't working for me.

Then, in Miami, through continuous dedication—the same dedication that I knew had helped me get to where I was—I was able to gain the coach's trust as a consistent player. I proved that I could be one of those fifty-three players that could go out on Sunday and make a contribution to help the team win.

VALUABLE PLAYERS MULTIPLY THEIR SKILLS

So, even though I'd been a top talent in Oregon, even though I'd been a top talent in the Big XII, those qualifications didn't necessarily translate to being a top talent in the NFL. The adversity I had dealt with earlier in my life—losing games and championships, injuries, surgeries, setbacks, changes, and other challenges or circumstances that didn't go my way— prepared me to deal with challenges later. I built upon those losses and was not shaken when circumstances did not go my way early on.

I have seen countless guys who make it to the league become disheartened after getting let go once or twice, and never find their way again. For me, though, making it through to Miami was a big stepping-stone. It was there that I was able to turn circumstances around. I saw what wasn't working, I built from there, gained the coach's trust, and showed that I belonged.

However, just because you're on the team one year doesn't necessarily mean you'll be on the team the next year. Perhaps you've seen the elaborate contracts that ESPN shows—a player signing for a big amount. Those people are few and far between on each team. A contract may stipulate a certain number years or a certain amount of money, but whether or not you are getting that time or that money is another story. Football is one of the pro sports where you're not necessarily going to get all the money that you signed for—unlike baseball or basketball.

So what did I need to do to continue to keep my status as a player on the team? I knew that they were going to go out and pick another player. Every single year, there's a new crop of talent coming up out of college. There were 255 more guys getting drafted and a boatload of other guys, just like me, who were not drafted and were even more hungry to prove that they belonged because they weren't picked.

So I said to myself, "I need to be multiple." I needed to find not just one way to be good and valuable—I needed to find three or four ways that my team could use me. I wanted to prove that they could use me here, over there, or back over here. I wanted to show that I could assume the role of a couple of other players as well as take on the tasks that I was already good at and could build upon.

LEARNING FROM MISTAKES TURNS LOSSES IN TO WINS

Throughout my career, I've brushed off complacency and pushed myself to become better. In high school, I knew I was good. Colleges were sending me letters, and people were talking to me, but no one was sending me the kind of scholarship offer that I really wanted.

❝ So it was time for something to change. I asked myself, "What do I have to do TO PROVE TO THEM that I deserve what I want? ❞

By going to camps with kids from around the country, I knew that, while I was good in Portland, there was also a good kid in Seattle. There were also skilled kids in Boise. There were kids in San Francisco, Las Vegas, and Los Angeles. You name the city, there were players there—and not just in my region, but across the country—who all wanted to go to the same place I wanted to go. I had to ask myself how I was going to stand out.

Standing out in high school to make it to college football is one thing. Standing out in college to make it to the pros is another. Less than 1 percent of college kids are going to make it to the pros and 0.01 percent make it from high school football to the pros. Considering the total number of high school football players out there, the chances of making it all the way to the big leagues are very, very minimal. So how do you continue to be one of the best?

The simplest way for me to stand out and become a better player was to intentionally reflect on and learn from my mistakes. When I lost or when I was unprepared, I took the opportunity to learn how to be prepared in the future based on what had happened.

In the same way, being continuously blindsided in business is not good. You don't want to be hit upside the head multiple times. You can't have someone come in and repeatedly take advantage of you through a caveat, a contract, a loophole, or a new market share.

Because I am from Beaverton and spent my childhood where the Nike world headquarters are, I hate to give this example, but it illustrates this point well. Under Armour created a nice, little niche for themselves when they came out with their Under Armour long-sleeved shirts to help keep athletes warm. Everyone said, "I need to make sure I have my Under Armour under my jersey." Every other kind of athletic wear on our bodies was Nike, but only Under Armour sold a product like its long-sleeved shirts. Soon, however, Nike caught on and came out with the Pro Compression, which was very similar to Under Armour's shirts. However, it took Under Armour coming out with it first before Nike made its product.

Nike learned from that experience, and, being as innovative as Nike is, they continued to evolve from there, and the whole episode wasn't a problem. It's important to note, however, that even a hugely successful company—Nike is a giant—couldn't keep someone else from finding a way to crack into their market. Ever since its creation of its long sleeve, Under Armour has been on the rise in the country and within multiple sports. It now has one of the top basketball names behind its shoes, which was probably not even a thought in their mind when Under Armour started.

It's impossible to stay number one at all times. Everyone wants to get to be the best and then remain in that spot, but—no matter what, even if you are the best in your industry—you will be blindsided at one point or another. When that happens, you need to be prepared to make small adjustments and bounce back.

Takeaways:

1. Avoid being blindsided by understanding your weaknesses.

2. Use losses as learning experiences. Don't dwell on them, but don't brush them aside. Make sure the same error doesn't happen twice.

3. Be multiple so you can make a quick shift or change when a blindside moment comes up.

CHAPTER 8

LEADERSHIP
MISTAKES

"There will be obstacles.
There will be doubters.
There will be mistakes. But
with hard work there are no
limits."

Michael Phelps

You're the leader, and you are in control. You are powerful and fearless. You're in the driver seat. You're the CEO, the director, the captain of the team.

What happens when things go wrong? What happens when someone on your team isn't performing well? What happens when a person criticizes you and your leadership ability? All of this will happen when the limelight is on you. Everyone is watching you, and the pressure is on for you to make decisions and to lead.

Leadership is stressful, and it's easy to make mistakes. I want to share with you a couple of costly leadership mistakes that, while having the potential to undermine you and derail your team, are easily avoidable.

LEADERSHIP MISTAKE #1: GIVING UP

The first mistake is giving up. Never, never, never give up on yourself, a coworker, or a player. Once you've given up on people, and especially if they know that you've given up on them, you've burned a bridge. That trust can never be rebuilt because you've shown that when it gets tough, you'll fold.

Say that there is a breakdown somewhere in your system. There is a need for a change. You have a choice: you can replace people right away, or you can put effort into helping develop people. If you've done everything you can to help teach and develop a certain person, and, despite your efforts, you feel like you can no longer work with this person, then, possibly, it is time to make a change with their role or job position.

But that's far different than what I mean by giving up and leaving people in the place where they are failing. Giving up on people means both losing faith in their ability to succeed on their own and also deciding not to put energy into helping them learn how to get to that place. If you've truly given up , then you need to let them go. If they know that you've given up on them, how are they going to work for you? They will not be able to give you their best work on a team that doesn't even believe in them. If people know that they're no longer wanted, if they know they are not being well received, you need to find a replacement.

> **❝ Cut your losses quickly and recognize the failure. ❞**

Own it, and either close the division or reposition personnel to be of better use. Don't give up on them.

More importantly, though, never give up on yourself. Giving up on yourself is something that I've seen many, many people do this, both successful and unsuccessful, and it always leads to that person's demise. I've seen people with talent far superior to my own—in athletics, in school, and in business—who have not achieved what they could have if they would just have kept going.

Giving up on yourself is something that you may not even notice that you're doing. I've seen this happen to many athletes. At first, when athletes begin to train, doing repetitions over and over and over, quick and rapid gains are made. Early on, you see great success from week to week—you see more and more development. The physical and tangible results are right in front of you. There comes a point, though, at which the rapid gains start to slow. Results aren't showing from day to day, or even week to week. You begin wondering, "Is there nothing more that I can do? Is this as far as I can go? Have I reached the plateau? Am I not going to get any better? Is this my maximum?" I definitely experienced this feeling of frustration and began to think about these questions.

The answer is no. Many athletes, especially the elite ones, will reach a point where there's very, very little return on their work. It's frustrating because you've seen yourself make huge gains. Maybe you greatly improved from your freshman year in high school to your junior in high school, or maybe your increase came during your college career—freshman year to junior year. Maybe you saw a dramatic change from your rookie season to your fifth season or your first year at the company to your fifth year at the company. It could be even within one year that you improved so much, and you expect that same curve to continue. You would, of course, like to make exponential gains over and over, but the reality is that this kind of repeated growth will probably not happen.

So as you're leading yourself or your team or your organization, realize that there may be a point of diminished returns. You, as the leader, may become a little disgruntled with the lack of progress. You have to stay the course here. If you do not stay the course, you will get off track to your goal, off the plan that you originally outlined. Know that these smaller results, these diminished returns that I'm talking about, are something that the most elite athletes in the world experience. Think of your favorite athlete, or the most successful person you know:

That person has experienced this same pattern. But successful people have also continued to stick with what got them to their success. They continue to build and find different ways that they can get better at their responsibilities.

It would be easy for me to give up on becoming fast. I realize that I've gotten to be about as fast as I can run. Of course, I am going to continue practicing and continue to strive to run faster. My speed has always been heavily criticized at every level I played. So I continue to work at it. I was never the fastest player, but that did not mean that I gave up on myself.

Instead of giving up, I started thinking of other ways that I could improve my play. Since it was getting tough to make gains in speed straight ahead, I worked on lateral speed and quickness. Most importantly, I worked on mental quickness, developing a sharp mind to be able to execute, react, and adapt quickly to whatever situation was thrown at me. This was important because if you can physically do a task but can't mentally execute the task in the moment, then you won't be able to get the task done.

> **ff You can only go
> as fast as
> # YOUR MIND
> can take you. 55**

In both athletics and in business, you need to continue to build and develop yourself. Never give up on yourself or allow others to see that you've given up on yourself. This is the single most devastating leadership mistake I've seen.

LEADERSHIP MISTAKE #2: LABELING A SITUATION AS IRREPARABLE

Secondly, do not assume a situation isn't fixable.

Certainly, some decisions are irreversible. If you make a transfer to a new organization, you obviously can't go back, although maybe you wish you could. Perhaps you've decided to go to a different team in free agency or you've taken a job and burned the bridge from your previous position. In some situations, you can't go back the way you came.

Those realities do not take away from the truth, though, that in most situations where problems have arisen, where leaders identify an issue, there are steps that can be taken to improve that situation. Realize that there's something you can do about a problem—there's something that can be fixed. Perhaps it's a personnel change that needs to happen; there's a staff issue where someone needs more training.

ff Perhaps you can
LOOK AT YOURSELF
in the mirror and see that
you can do something personally
about this situation;
maybe the **problem** started with **you. JJ**

Seek out problems diligently, and try to stop them as early as you can. Ultimately, it's important that you, as a leader, examine how the problem could have come from something you've done. People watch their leader and imitate their leader. Even if a problem isn't coming directly from you, maybe it has stemmed from actions which, originally, were patterns of behavior that you modeled for your employees or teammates. I've been in business with my brother for about two years now, and we have had our fair share of miscommunication. We've definitely made mistakes. Even though we are brothers, even though we know our goals, and even though our vision for our company is clear, there have still been a variety of situations that have gone poorly. It's been best when we address issues quickly, before heading too far down a wrong path. It's easiest to fix problems at the early stage, but recognizing you may be the problem can be a hard conclusion to arrive at.

Addressing a problem could be as simple as changing your communication style with a key employee or teammate who, for whatever reason, is off track in a certain area. Typically, people expect to see their employees and teammates every day in one location, but what happens if someone needs to work remotely or leaves to open up a new branch? How are you going to communicate? It should be similar to how you have been communicating so far. You don't want to let people think that their physical distance means that they don't have to communicate with you. When the reins are let a little loose, some people feel that they're on their own. Maybe they're opening up a new branch of the company, and they feel that they've learned everything already. Clearly, this is not true, and communication is still important. As a leader, you need to check in with them consistently. You've got to stay on the same page. Otherwise, after three months' time, you will check in and see that a small problem gone awry one day has grown into a big and daunting problem.

I harp on this example so much because I've experienced it. Things could be going well when together, then with expansion, gaps in communication and processes were exposed. Time lapsed without communication or updates; these are things that never would've lapsed when in the same location. But we were able to reverse this negative trend quickly because we were able to face reality, that we had made a bad decision and things needed to pivot in a different direction. Since making those changes, things have been significantly smoother!

Leaders everywhere love people who make themselves part of the solution instead of part of the problem, especially those who work towards a solution instead of harp on the problem. This was definitely true of many of the coaches in my career. As a leader myself, I don't want people coming to me with more problems. I'm sure many business executives feel the same way. If someone brings up a problem, leaders also want to see that this person has come up with a possible solution as well. Diligent employees have already asked themselves, "What can we do to get over this? How can we better ourselves? While we can't undo the problem, since it's already here, let's see how we can fix it."

Problems can be repaired. It's up to you, as a leader, to view them that way and to encourage your team to view them that way.

❝ You've got to adapt, overcome, and MOVE FORWARD. ❞

LEADERSHIP MISTAKE #2: PUTTING YOURSELF ABOVE THE RULES

Lastly, one of the biggest mistakes you can make as a leader is thinking that the rules don't apply to you. In my opinion, this is fatal to your ability as a leader.

When you act as if the rules do not apply to you, your hypocrisy undermines your authority. You are basically saying, "Hey, I'm going to lead, and I'm going to say a lot about how you should act and what you should do, but I'm not going to actually follow any of my own instruction." Why should you expect any of those people to follow you or listen to you?

Certainly, some people, intimidated by your important position or feeling threatened by your ability to fire them or blackmail them, will follow your rules no matter what. But there are going to be many people—when it comes to crunch time, when that little extra work or split-second decision matters, when you are counting on them to learn on their own—who will not put in the work. Why would they want to do that for a person who doesn't even follow their own rules? Especially as a leader, do not compromise company values or act in a way that is detrimental to your team. You want to model excellent behavior so that other people can imitate you.

If you can create a company, division, team, or group that has the integrity and skill to lead themselves as individuals, and if all of those individuals see you as a leader whom they can model their own work after, as a leader who has instilled character throughout the organization, then you have a chance for success. But thinking those rules don't apply to you is fatal. I've seen leaders make many mistakes. But these are three you don't have to let defeat you. When you find yourself in leadership and things get tough, don't give up. Continue training your team and working on yourself. When you encounter problems, find a way to fix them. Be creative and know that there are always steps that you can take to move forward. When you hit your stride, resist the temptation to be above your own company practices. Model the behavior you want to see spread in your group, and let the integrity of your organization bring you success.

Takeaways:

1. You are the one in charge. Act like it.

2. Don't give up on people. If they are not preforming, evaluate their strengths and find a place where those strengths will help them to be successful. It's your job to develop them.

3. Lead by example. The "rules" apply to you.

CHAPTER 9

YOUR PERSONAL
POWER
PLAYERS

"Losers assemble in small
groups and complain.
Winners assemble as a
team and find ways to win."

Bill Parcels

SUCCESSFUL PEOPLE HAVE SUPPORT SYSTEMS

A support system holds something together and absorbs tension—like a suspension bridge. Not only are support systems an important infrastructure for physical structures but also for organizations and for people individually.

> **ff** Everybody needs
> # SUPPORT IN THEIR LIFE,
> and that **support** can come
> from a **variety of sources. JJ**

In my life, I have been blessed with two parents. I was raised in a home with both a mother and a father who provided me support and were there for me daily. They are the people who I have constantly leaned on, throughout my life and to this day.

I know that some people aren't blessed with a big family, with two parents at home, or with parents at all, and need to find support elsewhere. I was also fortunate to find support in teachers, friends, coaches, and other influential people around me, including older peers. Supportive people, your personal power players, can come from a variety of places, but it is important that you have them. Having two to three people that you can lean on to help guide you through tough times—and to also keep you humble in the good times—is essential.

As I said before, and as you may know, nobody succeeds alone, and it's tough to succeed alone. If you're an entrepreneur wanting to do something different or unique, you know the struggle of feeling alone. That feeling is similar to when you get a holding call that brings back a game-winning touchdown or when you drop a game-tying pass. There are certain positions, in business and just in your personal life, where you find yourself in a lonely place. That's when it's important to have a support system in place.

POWER PLAYERS
PROVIDE PERSPECTIVE

Family has always been one of the most important parts of my life. Not only has having both parents there for me made a difference, but having two siblings there for me has also mattered. I mentioned that, in my life, I have looked up to older people, but the fact that my two siblings are younger than me has not kept them from being supportive. Even though I was the oldest one, I would always turn to them. I wouldn't necessarily talk through the details of my tough situations with them, but I definitely gained support and perspective just by being around them. They reminded me that, whatever I was facing, it wasn't the end of the world and there were other important parts of my life. It was always nice to know that, regardless of my performance on the football field, I had their support. Simply going on a boat and enjoying peace and quiet on the river with them was a release.

ff Your family can be a great
RESOURCE TO HELP YOU
when you **fall down,** when you **lose,** when something **goes wrong,** or when you need guidance. **JJ**

But I know, sometimes your family might not be an option for a support system.

Moving out to Kansas State for college, away from my family, was a big change for me. I did not know anybody when I arrived in the state of Kansas. I had visited the school once, so my arrival was only my second time being in the state, and I was eager to see what was in store for me. Within my first week of being there, though, I felt immensely homesick. It wasn't a good feeling, but I knew that I could call home whenever I wanted. When I talked with my family, they always reassured me that everything would work out. They would tell me that home was always there for me and not to worry. They encouraged me, reminding me that, while I could always come back home, I had a great opportunity in front of me in Kansas if I stuck with it.

Their support helped guide me through the first few weeks and months in Kansas. Even after I had made some friends and felt a little more comfortable in my new atmosphere, their support helped get me into the season. On from there, I was able to develop another support system with my new teammates that have since become some of my best friends, as well as coaches and other mentors in the area. It felt like I had another family there for me. This made my existing support system even stronger.

The feeling of knowing you have people who have your back can make taking a risk, starting a new venture, or moving somewhere new that much easier, because if all else fails, you still have your support system, no matter where they are.

POWER PLAYERS PROVIDE CAMARADERIE

Moving forward in my freshman year, I also relied more on the support of my friends who were going through similar situations. They, too, were freshmen in college for the first time, playing on the big stage, in the Big XII, in front of huge audiences at both home and away games. Anywhere from 50,000 to 100,000 people were in attendance to watch our games. We were all dealing with the pressures of workouts, going to class, studying for tests and exams, as well as practicing and studying for upcoming games. We had to manage our time well, and balance the different emotional ups and downs of school and being away from family. My network of friendships really helped me succeed early on. I knew that I wasn't alone. There were other people going through the exact same experiences as me. Because I didn't feel alone, I was able to focus on the valuable opportunities in front of me, to be present, and to continue my work.

Even when you may think that you're the only one out there, you're not. Someone else is out there having the same experiences as you, probably feeling the same way. Maybe that person who has felt the same way as you do also knows how to get through this experience. This person has made the mistakes you're making, they've felt the same discomfort that you are feeling, and they can help you get through your problems. Maybe, with their guidance, you'll solve everything in a week's time, instead of suffering for a year, two years, or maybe your entire career.

POWER PLAYERS
SHARE THEIR EXPERIENCES

Throughout my football career, I leaned on my coaches. I always loved learning from them, and not just from my dad, who was a coach, but also from coaches who had professional experience and coaches with unique backgrounds.

One of my coaches during my sophomore and junior years was an Italian man from a completely different part of the country. He had an accent that I'd only heard in movies—nobody in Oregon speaks the way that he did. He was someone completely different from me, but he was really someone that I could lean on. I relied on him to help me improve my game because he had come from the NFL, and he knew what it would take to get there. He could tell me how I could get to the pros, what to do, what not to do, and what the people at the next level would be looking for in me, particularly. Support like that was invaluable. I don't know where I would be without someone like him in my life.

My head coach, my offensive coordinator, and my position coaches on the K-State staff all were very supportive as well, always helping me discover what I needed to do and helping me get back on track when they felt like I was veering in the wrong direction.

POWER PLAYERS
STRETCH YOUR LIMITS

Education was a big part of my life. My parents were both teachers. In high school, I had a couple of teachers who would check in with me, and, in college, I had the same situation. These Kansas State professors cared about my academics and my success, and they were the ones who pushed for me to apply for the Rhodes Scholarship.

Before my recruiting trip, I had been unfamiliar with the Rhodes Scholarship. Our head coach at the time, Ron Prince, was certain that I could succeed both academically as well as athletically, and he mentioned this coveted scholarship to me. He told me that he thought I could be one of the rare people to play sports and win this award.

I applied for the scholarship as a junior. At the time, Kansas State, compared against other public schools, had the most winners of the Udall, Truman, Rhodes, and Marshall Scholarships. I felt that I could be one of these winners. Obviously, schools like Harvard and Yale and other private institutions had more winners, but because Kansas State was as successful as it was as a public institution, I had faith that I could get this scholarship. I had great support from a variety of academic staff at Kansas State who guided me through the application and interview process.

It was a one-of-a-kind experience. I interviewed with three of the winners from Kansas State that had won the Rhodes scholarship—a Truman winner, a Udall winner, and a Marshall winner—and a couple of other highly acclaimed academic professionals. It was the roughest interview of my life. I had never experienced anything as harsh or as intense as that interview. It was then that I realized how difficult it was to win this award. I was aware of the prestige, and I was not afraid of losing. I truly believed I had a lot to offer and could win, but this process helped me realize that there was much more to this award than I was expecting. I learned more about its reputation my senior year through coursework and different classes. Looking back, I wish I had run again in my senior year, having been through the experience once and being able to answer their questions with more precision and deeper thought the second time around.

Ultimately, I thank my mentors for encouraging me to step out into a situation that stretched my limits. They helped me move forward when I felt that I might be outclassed or maybe out of my league. I would not have been able to do it, though, without leaning on the guidance and knowledge of my personal power players.

POWER PLAYERS GIVE GUIDANCE

People can be there to support you in many different ways. They're not there for your popularity whatsoever.

They're there to see you succeed because they have faith, trust in you, and like you as a person—for who you are and what you stand for. They're also there to keep you on course when you waver or when they feel that you are straying.

When I was a freshman in college, I, like many students, made mistakes and got distracted. College presented me with new situations and more choices, and I was out on my own for the first time. There were definitely times when I had to deal with the consequences of my actions, whether I had participated in a food fight in the cafeteria or had not shown up to class on time. There were a few times I got involved in situations that could have snowballed—they could even have kept me from my goal of graduating and moving on to play professionally in the NFL. These events led to conversations in my coach's office or with dorm counselors who questioned me, my friends, and decisions that could have derailed my career in football entirely. But I was able to learn, lean on my support, and know what was right and wrong. I moved forward and learned from those experiences. What helped to get forward the fastest was sitting down and evaluating what decisions I made daily and if they helped move me closer to my goal as an NFL player. When your goals are clear, it makes decision making very easy.

It may sound corny, but I look at each person in my support system as a square on a quilt. That quilt keeps me warm during times I feel cold. There have been many times that I felt alone. I was the only Oregon kid playing out there at Kansas State, and there was no one that shared my upbringing or background. Feeling alone, though, forced me to the realization that I could relate to guys who moved from the Northwest or West Coast. I could connect with people who had parents for teachers or had a parent who was also their coach. I found some people who also took school seriously, who loved academics, and who loved to learn. I found people who loved to work hard, who really loved to get in the weight room and push. I had different people that I could relate to help push me in different parts of my life. These people became part of my quilt.

Don't get me wrong: Although these people challenged me, my power players weren't all serious business all the time. Some of the same people who helped push me to be a great football player were also the friends who helped me unwind and relax. I leaned on them for a good social experience. It was great to find people that, though from different parts of the country, loved the same card games as me or who loved to play Mario Kart on a Nintendo 64. Something as simple as that eased my mind and recharged me for another strenuous day in the gym, in the classroom, and on the football field. Those times of relaxation allowed me to go succeed.

Fast forward to today, I still speak with most of the same power players who helped me throughout my life, and I have added some new ones as well. My latest venture has been in business, and succeeding in this field is not something that can be done alone. From the beginning, it was an uncharted course for me. Up until that point in my life, I'd always had coaches directing me and telling me where to go, what to do on which day, what play to run on, what's down—basically what was right and what was wrong.

After starting my own business, I quickly realized that I didn't have someone telling me what was right and wrong. While I was doing what I wanted and feeling great about it, I knew I could move forward so much faster if I had the help of somebody else. So I've slowly accumulated a variety of people that have grown my business skills, similar to the way that I had mentors push me on the football field and in the classroom. My power players encouraged me to go out and have experiences that, while maybe making me feel uncomfortable, also stretched me to a new limit. They wanted me try something different. They wanted me to see if there was a new opportunity there or to find out if I needed to go in a different direction. They helped me learn from my experiences and apply that wisdom to my current situations.

If you're feeling alone, be sure to build your personal power player team and keep them there for you. And don't forget to return the favor by being there for them. People are much more appreciative of those who appreciate them. I could not be more appreciative of those who helped me get to where I'm at, those who have guided me forward and supported me—my family, friends, coaches, and mentors. I'm always thankful for what they have done, and I have not forgotten it.

Takeaways:

1. Build your support system with Personal Power Players.

2. Have a variety of Personal Power Players, not people who will just agree with you, but those who will push you to be your best.

3. Seek inspiration from within and never be afraid to find inspiration or guidance from an unorthodox source.

CHAPTER 10

BUILDING
LEADERS

"Leaders aren't born. They
are made. And they are
made just like anything else,
through hard work. And
that's the price we'll have
to pay to achieve that
goal, or any goal."

Vince Lombardi

There's a constant debate if leadership ability is something you're naturally born with or if it is a skill that can be developed. I believe in both. While some people may be more gifted naturally at being a leader, it is still a skill that constantly needs to be practiced, refined, and improved upon.

LEADERS GROW CONTINUE TO GROW

I believe that, to a certain extent, everyone has the ability to lead. Some people have natural talent and will become effective leaders quickly. These people have a higher ceiling of potential for their overall leadership success. When I went to Kansas State, the administration was adamant that I join the leadership program. Kansas State has an excellent leadership program with a long track record of success. Because of my position as an athlete, they thought that this program, in tandem with a business degree, could help build my leadership skills. At age eighteen, I wasn't convinced that it was necessary for me to join this program, but I now realize that even natural leaders can learn more and build their leadership skills.

Just as it is possible for people to learn new, best practices in their field, it is possible for aspiring leaders to cultivate leadership skills too. Those without natural talent might need to have someone else identify their leadership traits and where they should begin practicing. They might need help developing their leadership style. They might need public speaking training. But everyone can grow in these areas, and it's important for anyone who hopes to be a leader to make an attempt rather than just think they weren't born with it.

LEADERS SEE THEMSELVES AS LEADERS

The first step to creating a leadership structure and to building leadership within yourself is believing that you can lead. Whether you know yourself to be a natural-born leader, or even if you do not have any leadership qualities or traits, the first step is recognizing that you can lead. If you don't believe you can, then how the heck do you plan on getting people to follow you?!

Not everyone is destined to or wants to be the leader of a big organization, a Fortune 500 company, or team captain. Not everybody wants the spotlight or attention of those highlighted positions. Not everyone wants the responsibility of handling and dealing with multiple people. Everyone, however, has a place to lead. You can be a leader of a family as a parent, a leader of your brothers and sisters, a leader amongst friends, or just a leader of yourself on a day-to-day basis.

There are going to be many times where you're by yourself and facing a decision. These are times that will truly test what you believe about yourself and reveal how you see yourself.

> **ff** You'll need to
> # LEAD YOURSELF
> in a **positive** direction. **JJ**

I've faced many of those decisions myself. Many of my best leadership moments have happened behind closed doors when the lights weren't on and when nobody was watching. I made the decision on my own to spend an extra day in the weight room, to spend an extra day training, or to spend an extra day taking care of my body so I could perform when everybody was watching and the moment mattered most. I chose to study, learn something new, or meet new people. I never ran around bragging to everyone about all the extra time I spent training. The work would show itself later on. When the spotlight was on me, those decisions would come through in the ways that I conducted myself and in the ways I performed.

Seeing yourself as a leader means being able to discipline yourself. Perhaps you can pick up a little extra work on the weekend or on your off time. Realize that the clock doesn't just stop at five and that you might have to put a little more work in after hours or, at least, be a little more diligent while you're at work. Think of all the things that you can control to guide yourself in the right direction.

&& Being able to lead yourself
# CREATES CONFIDENCE
in your **vision of yourself** as a leader.
Then you'll be able to
go on and **lead others. JJ**

LEADERS SEE THEIR OWN STRENGTHS AND WEAKNESSES

So, after recognizing that you have the ability to lead and that you need to lead, where do you start? Identifying the leadership traits that you possess—your strengths and weaknesses—is a crucial first step.

Some people can have a natural leadership trait with their stature and size. Some people lead vocally, by what they say, or are louder than most, automatically drawing the ears of those around. Some people are great at encouragement and provide a positive spirit no matter the circumstances. Some people excel in all of these areas. Find out what it is that attracts people to you. Do you bring your teammates up when they are down? What essential role do you play in your group? If you were to leave, what would your coworkers miss about you? Maybe your diligence and work ethic are what make you stand out, and you can always be counted on to deliver. What do you possess that makes you a leader?

After taking a hard look at yourself to find your strengths and weaknesses, write them down. It is your strengths that have led you to your current position, and weaknesses that have held you back. Continue to build upon your strong suits. Practice them every opportunity you can, in creative and different ways. Maybe your strength is dealing with people, and you have had practice and success in dealing with people who are older than you. Take the strength of your people skills and develop them with your peers and with people younger than you. Maybe you have had success selling one product but do not know how to talk about another one. Take your communication strengths and apply them to a new product. Maybe there's an opportunity for you to practice leading a new group of people who have different skills than you or who come from a different background. However you can, continue to develop your strengths. Never neglect them and allow them to turn into weaknesses.

A strength of mine has always been communication. I can communicate with others equally no matter where they're from or how they were raised. Playing football while at Kansas State highlighted this strength. I played with guys from all over: New York, Virginia, Hawaii, Samoa, Florida, Texas, Kansas,

California, etc. There were people from all over with different ethnic backgrounds, financial upbringings, and religious views on our team, so being able to work with people different than yours was an essential skill for our players. We had to be able to communicate quickly, at the drop of a hat, and be able to lead one another to make plays and win games.

I quickly realized that I could excel at this kind of collaboration. I saw how important it was, so I continued to develop this skill. I listened to people who had a different perspective than I did, wanting to understand the "why" behind their perspective and what led them to that particular line of thinking or decision. I asked them how I could better communicate with them. I asked myself how I could better relate. Not that I had to identify with everyone on every level, but I wanted to be able to lead, and leading requires communication and having a deeper understanding of exactly who you're leading.

> **ff Identify what your strengths are and continue to practice and DEVELOP THEM IN different environments. 55**

See how your strengths translate with different audiences—with people from varying ages, cultures, financial backgrounds, and religious backgrounds. Do not limit your strength to a targeted area, but develop your skills to be all-around, well-developed strengths.

Next, work on your weaknesses. Find out what those are. What are you not good at? Where do you continuously breakdown? When do you find others not listening? Where do you find you need to be more versatile?

For me, I realized that I needed to be a little more vocal. I've always preferred to lead by example. Sometimes, though, leaders need to be the ones to step up and say something. You may need to confront somebody. You might need to explain what needs to be done in order to take the organization in the right direction. As a leader, you may need to be the one to have a strong vocal presence.

I continue to work on being vocal, and I still recognize it as a weakness of mine. However, I am much further along, having acknowledged this weakness and deciding to address it. Ignoring your weaknesses won't help you or anyone. You've got to be sure that you've pinpointed both your strengths and your weaknesses.

Leaders who want to grow in leadership will identify a need for leadership then seek areas for their own improvement, knowing they have exponential possibilities. Never settle for where you are now and continue to evolve and grow as a leader.

Takeaways:

1. Start with being able to lead yourself each day.

2. Identify your strengths and weaknesses as a leader; build upon strengths and practice weaknesses to become more well-rounded.

3. Continue to grow and find new ways to improve as a leader!

CHAPTER 11

THE POWER OF
WINNING

"I play to win, whether during practice or a real game. And I will not let anything get in the way of me and my competitive enthusiasm to win."

Michael Jordan

Winning is powerful. When you set out to do something, you want to win, don't you? I know I do. When I was a kid, I wanted to be the best at whatever I was doing. I wanted to win everything—even video games, card games, or board games. My college roommates, and even my friends from high school, know that even if the competition is ping pong or cards, I want to win!

Internally, everyone wants to win. Nobody likes losing. Nobody sets out to do a task and say, "Wow, I did so poorly, but I'm happy with that." Everyone wants to do something great.

Doing something great starts with the very first and smallest of wins. This chapter will discuss the power of winning and how one win leads to the next win, as well as how you can create and build your own momentum.

Momentum is a term often associated with sports. When I think about momentum in a football game, I think of how one play leads to another play, which leads to a big play which, potentially, leads to a touchdown. One drive feeds into the next drive, which feeds into the next. Each of these small pieces builds momentum throughout the game. The result of that game builds momentum going into the next, and so forth.

But how does momentum apply to the world outside of sports? I gave an example from a football game, and that same kind of progression happens with many different sports. But how can you use momentum when you're training or at work or in business? How do you create and build momentum?

For me, I realized that I needed to be a little more vocal. I've always preferred to lead by example. Sometimes, though, leaders need to be the ones to step up and say something. You may need to confront somebody. You might need to explain what needs to be done in order to take the organization in the right direction. As a leader, you may need to be the one to have a strong vocal presence.

I continue to work on being vocal, and I still recognize it as a weakness of mine. However, I am much further along, having acknowledged this weakness and deciding to address it. Ignoring your weaknesses won't help you or anyone. You've got to be sure that you've pinpointed both your strengths and your weaknesses.

Leaders who want to grow in leadership will identify a need for leadership then seek areas for their own improvement, knowing they have exponential possibilities.

❝ Never settle for where you are now and continue to EVOLVE AND GROW as a leader. ❞

Small wins are all over the place. Think about physical training. Everyone wants to get in the best shape and be the most physically fit person they can be. They want to look amazing, have a six-pack, lift the most weight in the gym, and run as fast as everybody else—or faster. But getting to this point doesn't happen overnight. In order to progress, you first have to lay out smaller goals. You have to accomplish these goals first. If the ultimate goal is getting into the best shape you can be in, you need to start with one workout, simply getting to the gym for the first workout; that alone is a win. Completing the entire workout plan, that's another win. Consuming the required amount of water, there's another win. You can see how many of these small wins are things completely in your control, allowing you to build up momentum from day to day without anyone else interfering or causing a loss. Ultimately, over time, these small wins build up and allow you to hit milestone goals and eventually reach the end goal. They make winning become a pretty simple process—NOT easy, but simple.

I'll use myself as an example and confess that after I finished playing football and started building my own business, I neglected working out for quite a while. It caught up with me. Soon enough, it had been so long, I had to change something. I realized that I needed to start my day doing something that I enjoyed—and, for me, that something was working out. Getting back in the gym for the first time was my first step to getting back into shape, which was what I wanted. Also, starting my day with something that I knew I was good at meant starting the day with a win. I started to intentionally begin the day with that small win to fuel the rest of my day and launch my day in a positive direction.

MOMENTUM STARTS WITH WIN #1

Of course, going to the gym one time wasn't going to get me what I was looking for. For you, too, one small win will not be enough. If you are looking to get in shape, you need to go in each day throughout the week, come again the following week, and then come in again the week after that. One day builds to another day, and those days build to a week, and those weeks build to a month, which build a quarter, which build half a year, then a whole year—before you know it, you've made a whole lifestyle change. You're consistently going into the gym, working out, doing what it is that you want to do, and setting yourself up to achieve your goals.

Creating that momentum can be tough, especially at first. It's hard to start. It's hard to get going. There are plenty of people out there who I know who want to lose five, ten, twenty, or even fifty pounds. For myself, the goal is twenty-five pounds, which isn't going to happen overnight and cannot happen in one week or maybe even one month. You really need to dedicate yourself to going into the gym every day. Let one good workout fuel the next and the next.

Maybe you're also like me and used to be much more fit and able to lift more weight, so going back to the gym may be depressing for you to see how far you've fallen physically. All of that negativity has to immediately go out the window! I let that consume me for the first couple of visits to the gym, but ultimately I reversed the train of thought. Instead of feeling dejected over having dropped so far, I realized that I'm capable of doing more and where I can get back to, since I had already done it before.

I set smaller, more realistic workout goals with weights and exercises I knew I could complete, but were also challenging. Results don't come when everything is easy, but wins are needed to fuel motivation and create positive momentum. I was doing less weight than the majority of the people in the gym, yet staying in my own lane because, hey, that's where I'm at today and this is my path towards accomplishing my own goals. Don't try to compare yourself to somebody else in this process!

I've also had to create momentum in school. I always wanted to be a great student and to have the best grades in the class. To me, it was just another area to compete. Your final grade, though, comes at the end of the term, semester, or trimester. Just as in athletics, you need to build up to your final grade.

You start the very first day of class by just showing up. Then, after showing up, break down your goals into smaller, achievable steps. Learn something that first day. Every day when you step into the classroom, make a point to have one takeaway. Then complete the homework. This is a cycle that can build upon itself. You've set yourself up in a routine. You can say to yourself, "I know the drill. I come to class; I'm present and giving my full attention. I learn one thing each day—if not, more—and then I do my homework that night, the next night, and the next." When a test rolls around, you don't have to study as hard because you've been present each day in class. You've paid attention. You've done your homework. You've asked questions. You've learned along the way. Note something every day that you can apply later to your final test, and when the final test comes, you'll be ready to give your best. You've applied yourself each day and built momentum in a series of small wins throughout the term. These wins will help you ace the test later.

The biggest challenge for me has been starting momentum in my business. I'm sure a lot of you who have started your own business can relate. Or maybe you are trying to build a team, lead a new division, launch a new product, or initiate a new marketing scheme. When you are the one responsible for generating most, if not all, of the momentum, it can seem daunting. In my business, we've had plenty of ups and downs, and, for us, the learning curve has been steep. Our company started as a twenty-six-year-old and two twenty-three-year-olds trying to revolutionize the way people receive injury and chronic pain treatment. We wanted to help people recover in less than ten days. This sort of business was brand new to the public—it had never been done before—so how did we get going?

We started by calling people. We brought them in to see if they liked the experience. We offered rewards for people who would tell their friends about us. Slowly, we developed a strong base of clientele who were experiencing the results that we promised. This group steadily referred in more people. This growth, though, could never have happened without the first phone call. Just picking up the phone can be hard. Having the first person come in, putting yourself out there, feels vulnerable. You worry, "Are they're going to like what I have to offer? Are they not going to like it? Is it going to be weird? Are they going to ask questions?"

But you have to start somewhere. Momentum begins when you gain the first win. And this first win has to come from you. It's a lot of pressure. I've often felt the pressure to perform, especially on the field. As a professional athlete, I felt that if I didn't make something happen, my team would not move forward. Even when I was a little kid, I can remember thinking to myself, "Hey, I need to make a play or we're not going to win the game. I need to make a play to get us going." Getting the ball rolling can be the most difficult part of the comeback or the win. But once it gets rolling, once you start gaining momentum, you'll be surprised what happens.

WINNERS USE MOMENTUM TO OVERCOME CHALLENGES

Of course, there are going to be challenges and obstacles. Even with losses, you can still build momentum and overcome obstacles quickly if you learn from your experiences. When you have a negative experience, learn what you can from that situation, so it doesn't happen again. When you have positive experiences, identify what worked, and continue to grow to accommodate those practices. Use every last bit of the potential that you gained through the win of the positive experience.

If there's something going on with your team and morale is low, ask yourself what you can do. How can you turn things around? You can start with something very small like recognizing that people showed up. Acknowledge that everyone completed their assigned tasks. Maybe the work didn't generate a direct revenue right that day, but everyone was there, and everyone completed their work, and you recognize everyone for doing a good job. Then the next day, recognize people again. The next day, repeat the same process. You're starting to build up morale—a little bit at a time. That small sign of positivity, over the course of some time—perhaps a week or two weeks—models a positive attitude. That positivity spreads. It may spread quickly or it may take a long time, but that positive morale will accumulate. And all of that started with an intentional choice and strategy on your part.

Sometimes there were days on the practice field when I just did not feel like spending the next few hours banging my head against someone else. Some days, I did not feel like putting in the work. Football is a very emotional game. Along with being physically challenged, a player has to have mental toughness to deal with the tremendous mental strain. If you are not present in the game, emotionally and mentally, you will not be able to perform physically.

Because of this, you've got to keep morale high on a football team. So I—and many other people, coaches, teammates, and others in the organization—would sometimes come out to practice making some noise. We'd hoot and holler. We'd yell a little bit and try to get people excited when they were tired. Even though the other players knew we weren't really excited either, our artificial excitement multiplied to more artificial excitement, which turned into real excitement and enthusiasm. Suddenly, the whole team would be caught up in the cheers, and we were ready to be present for practice—physically, mentally, and emotionally.

The same process can happen at your work. Whether or not you are genuinely excited about what needs to be done, someone needs to model excitement, and you, as the leader, should be the one to initiate it. You are creating a small win, and that win can generate a little bit of momentum. Recognize that small win and build on it each day.

Don't ever be discouraged. Keep building upon one win to the next and, if you're having trouble starting off, start with the very smallest achievement possible. Like I said, it could be something as small as showing up with a smile on your face and showing up the next day, again, with a smile on your face—and the next day and the next day. Soon enough, everyone will start to show up with smiles on their faces. They're ready to work—work hard and do well. That excellent work may translate into the most successful product launch ever or even into the generation of millions of dollars in revenue.

You can start with a very small win and, with momentum, build from one win to the next. Build on that momentum day-to-day, month-to-month, quarter-to-quarter, year-to-year, and, pretty soon, you'll have a well-oiled powerful machine. You'll steamroll right over competition into a leading position.

Takeaways:

1. Winning fuels momentum. Build or rebuild momentum by starting with the smallest of wins and recognizing them.

2. Steam-rolling momentum doesn't build up immediately, it is a series of wins (and learning experiences from losses) over time that fuel the charge.

3. Never be afraid to initiate the momentum swing!

CHAPTER 12

MOVING CHAINS FOR CHANGE

"If you want things
to change, you must
change."

My head coach in college, Ron Prince, who's now the offensive line coach for the Detroit Lions, used to recite this quote to our team. It's a quote that has always resonated with me. As I think back on my football career, during college but also before and after college, I can see this principle reflected:

> **If you want things to change, you must CHANGE.**

STEP 1: EMBRACE CHANGE

The first step in the process of change is acknowledgement and acceptance.

In high school, I was unhappy with my options for the future. I felt that I was one of the best kids on my high school team, in the area and in the state. I didn't have multiple colleges— colleges that I wanted to go to, at least—knocking at my door or calling me telling me how much they wanted me or to offer a full scholarship.

So I continued to work, to put in time in the off-season, and to train while others, my friends, would go off and have fun after school. I can count on two hands the number of times I left school directly to do something with my friends instead of going to work out or going to a practice. If I wasn't playing football, I was playing basketball, and if I wasn't playing either of those, I was training for some upcoming event in one of those two sports (camp, tournament, showcase, etc.).

It was frustrating to be working while my friends were having fun, but I knew I was making good decisions. I realized that if I stuck with the program, if I trusted the system, if I believed in what I was on track to do, if I continued to be dedicated and to sacrifice, an opportunity would present itself. The opportunity would come through for me, and I would eventually get the scholarship I felt I long deserved.

Just as I had hoped, opportunity finally came when Coach Prince knocked at my front door with the news that Kansas State wanted to offer me a full athletic scholarship. Since I was an Oregon kid, this was a unique opportunity. No one else on the Kansas State team was from Oregon. I actually really wanted to go to the University of Washington or Stanford, but neither of them wanted me and neither of them had approached me about a scholarship. So this opportunity that I had worked for came to me in the form of a choice to leave my hometown, leave my family, leave Oregon, leave the Northwest, and leave the west coast for a place that I'd never been in my life. I didn't know anybody at Kansas State except for the tight end coach, who'd come to my house once, and the head coach, who'd also once visited. I had to choose whether or not I would embrace this change in my vision for my future.

But even though I had never expected to go to Kansas, I realized that if I wanted to get to my goal, my larger goal, of making it professionally, I needed to take this step. I knew that sometimes people have to change locations to advance in their career. This was how I made it to Kansas State to hear Coach Prince say, time and time again, "You know, if you want things to change, you must change." It was absolutely the right choice.

As I invested in this change over the course of my college career, I watched my own personal growth. It was rewarding to notice that the time I put in, which increased from freshman year to sophomore year to junior year, led to playing time, which also increased. I began experiencing more individual statistical success, I started to get a better feel for the game, and I actually performed better in the classroom. I finally felt comfortable where I was. Like I said, Kansas was a brand new place for me—a different part of the country with a completely different culture. I've never lived next to farm fields and cattle-grazing grounds or known people who enjoyed that life or even heard people talk about it. Going out there was just a whole new experience for me. But as I spent time there, I slowly felt myself become more and more comfortable within my role and my place at Kansas State.

Change isn't always bad. Most people are afraid of change—some are absolutely terrified of change. I mean, my parents could tell you, I was excited to go to college, but at the same time I was scared because I was not familiar with where I was going. I didn't know anybody there. It wasn't a good feeling. I'm sure some of you, who have been assigned a new role or transferred to another place where you didn't know anyone, can relate.

What I'm saying is that you can be successful as long as you accept the change. All this begins with acknowledging change and choosing to be present. Know that your circumstances will feel a little different and be okay with that. Embrace the change.

STEP 2: ADVOCATE FOR CHANGE

The second way to treat change, after embracing it, is to become its advocate. When you get on board with change, you've internally accepted that your situation is going in a new direction, and the next step is to be an advocate for that change within your team, group, or company.

I dealt with many different organizational changes throughout my career. I had two different head coaches in college. I had four different offensive coordinators and three different tight end coaches during my time at Kansas State alone. Professionally, I played for three different head coaches, four different tight end coaches, and four different offensive coordinators. Year to year change is not easy. But the best way to handle it is to support what the new leader is looking to do and to move in the new direction. Whether the new vision is for just the tight ends, for the entire offense, or for the entire team, embrace it and support it.

Fighting the new vision, combatting it by trying to bring situations back to the way they used to be with the previous leader—where you were comfortable—will not help anything. Change is going to happen. New leadership has been brought in to do something new with the program. The person is expected to make a change and go a new direction because that's what the company wants. There's a reason behind change.

You might be able to sabotage the situation if, after continued failures, the organization blames the new leader for a lack of success. You might feel that you have accomplished your goals. But is that really what you want? Do you want to be known as the cancer or the poison of the team? Do you want to be known as someone who's going to fight new leadership or new management? That's not what you want.

You might not always agree 100 percent with new change. Getting on board with a new direction and being okay with it is something that may take some time for you, individually. Continuing to resist the change, though, will not help you individually or help the group, team, division, or organization. By doing this, you will only stall and prevent success.

After a couple of months of being at Kansas State, I realized that the organization was trying to make some big changes. The team was just coming out of a period of mediocre performance. Even though I had just graduated, they were already giving me and other freshman multiple opportunities to prove ourselves on the field. At that point, most of us were new. There were a lot of incoming players, and we needed to work together—to click and be on the same page. We didn't come together immediately, and it was not funny to watch us struggle. Both the program and the players were reeling from change.

But I believed what Coach Prince kept telling us: that if we wanted things to change, if we wanted our win-loss numbers to change, then we must change. It was at this point that I made a decision to advocate for Coach Prince's leadership and to try to get others on board as well. I wanted to help turn this program around and restore it back to Big Twelve prominence, and I knew that we must put in more work as a team. We would have to sacrifice a little more of our free time to get in a few extra reps, to perfect our timing and to get to know each other. So I had to encourage our team in that direction.

The faster you can adapt and learn to grow with change, the better your life, individually, can become, and the more success you can have as a group, division, or team.

STEP 3: BE THE CHANGE

What happens if you keep coming up short, individually, or if the team, group, or division keeps failing? What if, even after change, things keep going wrong, or you keep missing goals, missing targets, missing bonuses over and over and over? What if, even after new leadership, you experience continuous losses? What must happen then?

Like coach said, if you want things to change, you must change. The way I always understood the quote, and what I believe my coach meant when he repeated it, was that if you're unhappy about something going on in your life, you need to stop complaining and start doing something about it. You're unhappy with your grades; you're unhappy with your position on the team; you're unhappy with your pay; or maybe you're unhappy with your life at home. Many people do not want to actually do anything about their problems—they'd rather post about them on social media. They want to talk to other people about their dissatisfaction and bring them down to the level of complaint. I'm guilty of this too at times.

❝ But if you really want things to change, you've got to stop talking about your situation and do something TO CHANGE IT. ❞

Comb through what's going on. Look systematically at what is currently happening. Find out what it is not working right for you, your team, your organization, and make small changes that create small wins and get your team back on the winning track.

Things don't get better by continuing the same way. Think of how people used to go into their home to talk on the phone, a phone that was attached to the wall in a stationary position. People were accustomed to making phone calls this way. Now people don't even have home phones anymore. People rely on their cell phones—a piece of glass that is their own, personal phone. Technology will develop, and change will continue to happen around you. You need to be able to adapt to those changes as well as make your own changes.

Get help if you can. Have someone with an outside perspective take a look at your organization to find what you are missing. You might be too close to the situation to see where you need extra help. For years my dad has been an outstanding coach for both football and track and field, but I never listened to him when he encouraged me to run track and field. I ended up struggling with speed throughout my football career. I kick myself now for not taking his advice. Now I know that most of the guys I played with in the NFL who were fast also ran track. Running wasn't a skill that I was naturally great at, as I've shared multiple times already, so listening to that bit of advice from my dad would have been helpful.

There were also times, though, that my dad's perspective was not enough. I needed more outside perspectives than just his. Although I trained with my dad throughout high school, and even in college and in the pros, he could not make me as fast as I needed to be. Once I got into my junior year, my dad finally realized that, while he could continue to help me with strength training, I needed to see someone else to work on my speed.

My dad won State of Oregon's State Track Coach of the Year four times at the highest division, won multiple titles, and won hundreds of meets with his girls' teams. He was a well-qualified coach. All that aside, it was time that I needed an outside look at my own individual skills. We hoped that someone else would see more of my problems and breakdowns. Luckily, I found those people, and I was able to fine-tune some of my skills and make improvements. Part of this success I owe to having someone else look at what was going on with me. Combine that new perspective with my constant drive to be better, and my game continued to evolve.

So don't be afraid to have someone else take a glance at your work. As the leader of the group, you must find solutions and find ways to get to your goals. If that means personal change, then seek that change, whatever the cost. Have other people look to find where you can try something new. Look at all the ways that you're attacking the current problem and see where the breakdowns are.

Dealing with change is difficult. If leaders in the group can adjust to change, work for change, and improve themselves, then the team, as a whole, will succeed.

Throughout my career as an athlete, I learned a lot about leadership. Through my disappointment in Little League, while being on my dad's team in high school, during my transition to collegiate play, throughout my experiences at Kansas State, and especially in my professional career, I grew. Each phase shaped me as I put in work, made mistakes, and made adjustments. Even today, I'm continuing to learn and develop my leadership through my business. As I've learned from the wisdom of others, I hope to pass on my own. The world needs excellent leaders in all areas of life.

❝ I hope you rise to the challenges of leadership, persevere through adversity, and lead your team to greatness, STANDING TALL. ❞

Takeaways:
1. Acknowledge and accept the process of change.

2. Be an advocate for the new vision.

3. Nothing will change until you change.

CURSED BY
EARLY
SUCCESS

"Always be prepared. Life is
full of the unexpected."

Early success is great. It's what you strive for. It's what you set out to do, succeed. The only reason you're doing something is to win and do well at it, so what's wrong with the success you asked?

Well, early success can be detrimental for a lot of things in a lot of people. A lot of people think that early success is something they're entitled to. They work for two weeks, made a big sale, closed a big deal, and that's what's going to happen for them as they move forward throughout the rest of their career. Wrong.

Early success, people win a championship, get hired as the highest recruit, enter college after choosing from a variety of top tier programs, after many coaches. Hall of Fame coaches even visited their house and told them how great they were. It means that they're destined for excellent success to the next level, right? Wrong.

Early success, a guy following from his high school years had been the number one recruit got to college, was a Heisman Trophy winner, gets drafted in the first round of the NFL. Is he destined for early success? Not necessarily so.

My point being here is that early success is not necessarily a precedent of future success. It does teach you to learn from what got you there and continue to build, but it also can be a very, very large area for complacency to set in, and complacency can be a killer to your growth as a person, player, leader or business executive.

Early success is something that you celebrate happening. The occurrence is awesome, "I feel great. I've succeeded. I've closed my big deal. I've got my first large account."

We've talked about the power of winning. That is simply a momentum-accruing event. You've done great. Now, continue to press for the next one and the next one and the next one. Follow what got you there for the first one and build on to the second one.

One thing that people continue to learn on, especially for football players, is that when something goes right, it never went as well as you thought it did. There's something you can learn from it. There's something you can take away to develop further for the next time.

What is it that you need to focus on to make that even better? What if that deal that only took two weeks could have taken one week? How would that affect you in the long term, in the long run?

Well, if you're taking two weeks for every deal, which could be outstanding depending upon what you're selling, what if you could take one week? Now, you've doubled the amount of deals you could close in one year, hit a new bonus, get a new promotion, and you get the point.

Someone that has been thought of as a high-quality, high-caliber athlete at a young age, maybe they are told that they're the best as early as ten years old, and they continue to develop and grow and be the best until age eighteen, but then what happens when they go off to college? They've been told they were the best. They've been nurtured by their community there around. Maybe they've played in some sort of national tournament or camp to get and deserve that recognition, but are they going to build upon it at the next phase, or do they just expect something similar?

My most fatal point with early success, along with the complacency, is the fact that people that have a lot of early success think that they're entitled to more. No one is ever entitled to success. It is something that is always worked for. Either someone ahead of you has worked for you and paved the way for you, because I know some people do get a few things here and there handed to them, but continued, sustained high-caliber, elite success is something that has continuously worked for or someone is always seeking development and continuing to evaluate what got them there, what will continue to help them grow and what has been the mistakes in the past.

So early success may be good, it may be bad. Don't be another one of those statistics of someone who did so well at a young age or early in their career and then failed to continue to grow and develop into their later years. There's always something you can take away from a situation, whether it's good or bad, fast or slow, big or small.

Find out what the key elements and key detailed points are in how you can work to overcome those, sharpen them up, fine tune and continue to build off that success and keep winning and creating that momentum that is so powerful in building a strong career.

JERON MASTRUD

ABOUT THE
AUTHOR

Education has always been at the forefront of Jeron Mastrud's priorities. Being born the son of two teachers, he graduated high school with a 4.02 GPA. In addition to his academic success, Jeron excelled at 2 varsity sports. The combination of both athletics and academics garnered recognition of several Ivy League schools.

Deciding on Kansas State University for his college career, he attended on a full athletic scholarship.

Jeron's success continued both athletically, philanthropically and academically. He set the record for most receptions by a tight end in Kansas State history, earning AP 1st Team Big XII honors, as well as 2nd Team All American. He spent time as a mentor to troubled middle school students and read books to children in elementary schools. He had an active role in the Kansas Special Olympics. After graduating cum laude in the winter of 2009, it was time for Jeron to pursue his dream of playing in the NFL.

In 2010 he signed with the Tampa Bay Buccaneers as an undrafted free agent. He was released in September of the same year. Immediately following his release, he spend two days with the New England Patriots, before being let go yet again. On his way to the airport, he received a call from the Miami Dolphins and this is where he would spend the next three years. He finished his NFL career starting 22 games, including the entire 2013 season for the Oakland Raiders where he also was a team speaker and guest captain.

Before leaving the Raiders, Jeron founded Pacific Neuro Therapy, a company which helps people overcome injury or eliminate chronic pain in 10 days or less.

As CEO of the Pacific Neuro Therapy, Jeron's overseas business development, expansion and direction of the company. He also has co-founded Reyes de la Tierra, an agricultural real estate company and Jet Resorts, a vacation rental home company.

Inquiries to book Jeron for speaking engagements can be made via email – team@JeronMastrud.com